The Singing School Handbook

How to make your school sing

Michelle James

Love learning, start singing

FABER *ff* MUSIC

© 2018 Faber Music Ltd and Sing Up Ltd
First published in 2018 by Faber Music Ltd
Bloomsbury House
74–77 Great Russell Street
London WC1B 3DA
Cover design by Susan Clarke
Page design by Adam Hay Studio
Illustration by Lauren Appleby
Printed in England by Caligraving Ltd

ISBN10: 0-571-54072-4
EAN13: 978-0-571-54072-3

To buy Faber Music publications or to find out about the full range of titles available
please contact your local music retailer or Faber Music sales enquiries:
Faber Music Ltd, Burnt Mill, Elizabeth Way, Harlow CM20 2HX
Tel: +44 (0) 1279 82 89 82   Fax: +44 (0) 1279 82 89 83
sales@fabermusic.com   fabermusicstore.com
For more information about Sing Up visit www.singup.org

FOREWORD

A Singing School is a place not just where singing happens regularly, but where all children are involved in singing, every day, as a normal part of school life. Singing is not on the periphery of school life but right in the middle of it. It is a place where the whole school community knows and can describe what difference singing makes to their school.

This book is a 'how-to' guide to help teachers and singing leaders working within school settings take appropriate steps towards making their schools Singing Schools. It has been written on the basis of 10 years' experience of doing this work within primary schools (for children aged 4–11) in the UK but our hope is that many of the principles and suggestions are universal enough and rooted simply in solid education pedagogy to be transferrable to other settings and to countries other than the UK even though the education frameworks and infrastructure may differ.

In 2007, the UK Government announced that there would be funding for a National Singing Programme for all primary schools in England. The programme was named Sing Up and given the strapline 'Help kids find their voice'. During its five years of funding Sing Up reached almost 100% of the 20,000 primary schools in England, trained more than 56,000 teachers and vocal leaders, set up a network of 30 Area Leaders around the country and created an online resource of 500 specially arranged and commissioned songs for young and developing voices.

Sing Up's overall aim is for every child to take part in high-quality singing activity every day. As well as this, Sing Up endeavours to:

- Raise awareness of the value of singing.
- Provide a comprehensive singing resource for children and singing leaders.
- Build and develop a committed and effective workforce to lead singing in and out of the classroom and the school, including young leaders.

Since 2012, Sing Up has been operating as a stand-alone organisation funded through schools' subscriptions to an annual Membership package. As well as continuing to work with primary schools, Sing Up now also works in secondary schools and internationally. In 2017, to mark its 10th birthday the organisation launched the Sing Up Foundation, a charity focussing on singing for children with special educational needs and disabilities; teenagers and mental health; and singing for older people to help improve lung health and for those with dementia.

Sing Up has been recognised with the Royal Philharmonic Society's (RPS) Education Award, the Making Music Sir Charles Groves Prize, The Smarta 100 Awards for social impact, nominations for Best Digital/Technological Resource and Best Musical Initiative in the Music Teacher Awards, and by the National Plan for Music Education. It's cross-curricular tools and support put singing at the heart of school life, building the benefits of singing into teaching throughout the whole school day. Sing Up will enable you to cultivate strong communities and healthy, happy and confident students.

A significant plank of the strategy has been to define and create Singing Schools around the country – to make every school a Singing School. Sing Up's definition of a Singing School is as follows:

- All pupils sing every day.
- The whole school sings together at least once a week.
- Singing regularly takes place in and outside the classroom.
- At least two people in every school are confident to lead singing throughout the school.
- Pupils sing in regular performances to internal or external audiences, and in recordings.
- The school recognises the value of singing as part of the school's culture.
- The head teacher, governors and staff are supportive of singing.

Steps to becoming a Singing School

Sing Up's framework for becoming a Singing School has been devised in consultation with arts education professionals, classroom teachers and music teaching specialists. It has three levels – Silver, Gold and Platinum. The Singing School framework guides schools on a journey towards becoming a Singing School and supports the head teacher and school community to discover the wide-ranging benefits of singing for themselves whilst developing high-quality singing and vocal leadership.

Sing Up's framework is designed to be accessible to all schools for children aged 4–11. This includes SEND (Special Educational Needs and Disabilities) schools which may incorporate a wider age range. It can be extended to include children up to age 13 or beyond and we have included some guidance on voice-change during adolescence to help with this.

Chapters 2, 10 and 11 (shaded grey) within this book contain the specific criteria for each level (Silver, Gold and Platinum) along with guidance and planning tools to help you get there.

The Song Bank

The Song Bank is Sing Up's extensive library of songs that can be used by any Sing Up Member to teach with in their school. Throughout the book, you will find Song Bank suggestions, that give you appropriate Song Bank songs to use for each activity.

About the author

Michelle James is the Chief Executive of Sing Up. Michelle originally trained as a violinist and singer and has a degree in Music and English Literature. She has worked within music education for the past 25 years in a conservatoire, an examinations board and a charity funding music-making for children and young people with least opportunity. She is passionate about the value of music and singing for everyone, particularly children. Michelle has been involved with Sing Up since its inception in 2007 and has been the CEO since 2011.

Terminology

This book is for all classroom teachers and vocal leaders – music specialists and non-specialists alike. The language and terminology used is intended to be easily understood by a non-specialist, whilst not patronising to a trained musician.

There are a number of UK-centric terms used throughout the book regarding the UK school system and music notation:

Primary school	School for children between the ages of 4 and 11
Secondary school	School for children between the ages of 11 and 16
Key stage	One of the five fixed stages of the English national curriculum
Senior leadership team (SLT)	The members of staff responsible for the management of school policy, targets, curriculum and welfare.
Continued professional development (CPD)	Training undertaken by professionals to develop and enhance their abilities.
Quaver	Eighth note
Crotchet	Quarter note
Minim	Half note
Semibreve	Whole note

Acknowledgements

This book has been a delightful project to work on with colleagues from Sing Up and Faber Music and experts from across the sector and there are many people to thank for their contributions:

For their patient and generous help with writing the text:
Shelly Ambury, Amy Armstrong, Stuart Barr, Lucinda Bristow, Sophie Gray, Charlotte Law, Beth Millett, Jenni Parkinson, Aimee Toshney, Emily Tully and Jenevora Williams.

For their previous contributions to Sing Up content from which we've drawn:
Catherine Andrews, Martin Ashley (and special thanks to OUP for their kind permission to reference Martin's book *Singing in the Lower Secondary School*), Celi Barberia, Elena Browne, Alison Daubney, Leonora Davies, Richard Frostick, Will Green, Bethan Habron-James, Mia Vigar, Graham Welch, Evangelos Himonides, Jane Werry and Katherine Zeserson.

For their help in the creation of the Sing Up Awards scheme:
Baz Chapman, Kate Gibson, Howard Goodall, Annika Joy, Andrea Pierides and Bridget Whyte.

For their outstanding commitment to the Sing Up Awards and the guidance and support they have given schools in achieving them: Amy Armstrong, Leonora Davies, Geraldine Gaunt, Pamela McGahon and Kathleen Still.

For permission to reference their insightful articles:
Clemency Burton-Hill (writing for BBC Culture online) and Ivan Hewett (writing for The Telegraph).

For support and guidance for Sing Up:
Darren Henley, Richard Hallam, Marc Jaffrey, Angela Ruggles, Matt Griffiths, Richard King, Christina Coker, Andy Parfitt, Anthony Sargent, Richard Stilgoe, David Sulkin.

Special thanks go to Tom Dent and Lesley Rutherford from Faber Music for their hard work and support and to all the team at Sing Up, as always, for their commitment, passion and immense sense of fun whilst working extremely hard!

And a final very special thanks to the Sing Up Board for their never-ending wisdom and energy:
Katherine Zeserson, Kathryn Knight and David Clarke.

CONTENTS

1

WHY BECOME A SINGING SCHOOL?

Becoming a Singing School motivates the whole school community to work together towards a common goal while taking part in an activity that everyone can do and enjoy – singing. Singing improves learning, confidence, health and social development. It has the power to change lives and help build stronger communities.

Take a moment to think about an ideal school environment. You might imagine a calm, well-operating and friendly, happy school, where:

- Children feel welcome, safe and secure
- Children arrive focused, enthused and ready to learn
- Children support each other's learning
- Learning achievements are joyfully celebrated by the wider school community
- Learning challenges are met with determination, optimism and self-belief
- There is a strong sense of teamwork in each class and across the school among staff and pupils alike
- Children are attentive listeners and productive learners
- Children and staff take pride in their school
- There's a strong community ethos in the school
- Behaviour and attendance are good
- Newcomers to the school are welcomed and integrated quickly
- Children with additional needs are supported, valued and included
- Parents, carers and the wider school community feel part of the school and are positive about its achievements and ethos.

Embedding regular singing into school life is a way of ensuring that all these attributes develop over time. At Sing Up, we have seen countless examples and collected many case studies where the school community themselves believe that it is singing that has transformed their school. From head teachers to pupils and parents, all have reported the change they have seen take place as the result of regular singing happening in the school. You will find examples of these case studies throughout the book.

"Singing threads through the life of this school and has created a positive ethos around the whole school. Our results are the result of the music that threads through the school."

Ann Golding, Head Teacher, Highfield Infants School

"The students have gained so much from music and singing beyond just the singing itself."

Stephen Whittle, Principal, Hayes School

Looking at it the other way around, it is uncommon to find schools where these 'ideal' factors are present and where there is no school commitment to singing, music or another art form. The creative arts – music in particular – are known to have a powerful positive impact on the school environment and on learning outcomes for pupils. And of the musical activities that you can embed in your school most readily and inexpensively, singing is the most accessible of all, and also the most adaptable and versatile.

Singing inspires, supports, develops and stimulates

There are many different benefits that arise from engaging in singing activities. These apply to all ages, from childhood into adolescence and through into retirement age and beyond. Almost without exception, everyone has the potential to sing competently and enjoy singing across their lifespan. Childhood provides a crucial opportunity to lay the foundations of a positive lifelong singing (and musical) identity and if nutured appropriately, singing competency will improve and improve.

The benefits of singing are now much better understood and documented in a range of academic and medical research and broadly break down into five categories:

1. Physical benefits
2. Psychological benefits
3. Social benefits
4. Musical benefits
5. Educational benefits

In combination, the benefits which fall under these five categories suggest that singing is one of the most positive forms of human activity. Here are several ways in which your school and students can benefit from singing:[1]

It has a remarkable impact on your health.

- One in eleven children receives treatment for asthma in the UK (Asthma UK, 2011). Singing helps strengthen respiratory and cardiovascular health.
- Singing helps stimulate the brain. It literally lights up more areas of the brain than any other activity.[2]
- Singing increases alertness and improves physical posture.
- Singing reduces stress and enhances the immune system.[3]
- Singing (healthily) is good for the voice and larynx.

It supports children's learning.

- Singing aids memory retention and helps children to retain new information and facts.
- Singing can help children improve reading skills.[4]
- Singing can increase enjoyment and participation across the curriculum.

It helps develop confidence and self-esteem.

- People feel good when they sing. Children who are good at singing feel good about themselves and are more socially included.[5]
- Singing is an inclusive, collaborative activity. It increases confidence, improves social cohesion, promoting tolerance and acceptance of others.
- Our voice is part of our identity; a confident, healthy voice links to a positive concept of self.

It builds communities.

- Singing is an inclusive activity that can bring a school community together like no other.[6]
- Singing is universal regardless of age, gender, language or ethnicity.
- Group singing maximises our potential to communicate with others using our voices.
- Performing helps to build confidence and encourage teamwork.
- Singing allows children to make a positive contribution to their class and school communities.
- Singing can help you learn to work as a team as well as valuing the contributions of individuals.

We asked teachers and head teachers what contribution singing makes to their school, here's what they said:

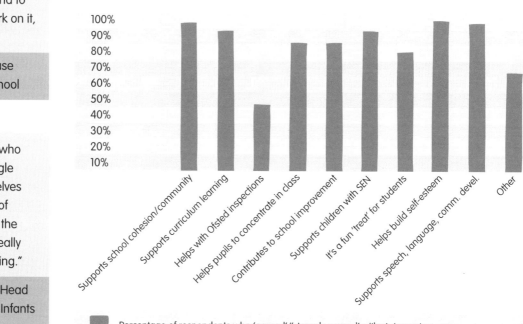

Percentage of respondents who 'agreed'/'strongly agreed' with statement

> "I've had parents say to me 'oh my child's reading has improved so much since they started choir'."
>
> Catherine Andrews, Highfield Infants School

> "[Singing] actually builds children's confidence so much and it makes them think if I set my mind to something, if I work on it, then I can do it."
>
> Deputy Head, Chase Bridge Primary School

> "You see children who are shy and struggle to express themselves grow... the sense of community within the schools is I think really enhanced by singing."
>
> Lynne Thompson, Head Teacher, Trafalgar Infants School

The most important factor

The numerous benefits of singing are often split into two groups – intrinsic and extrinsic. Extrinsic benefits include things like:

- Cognitive development – building neural pathways in the brain
- Language acquisition
- Memory and learning aids – supporting the learning of facts and concepts
- Teamwork and collaboration
- Increase in self-esteem and confidence
- Health benefits – neurological, respiratory and immunological as well as psychological

While intrinsic benefits include:

- Learning musicianship skills
- Becoming a better singer
- Creating a high-quality artistic output or performance
- Boosting mood and general positivity – feeling better when you sing
- Enjoying an artistic, expressive and creative experience for its own sake

The question remains, which is more important: that children are learning and progressing as singers, musicians and artists (intrinsic), or that they are participating in a team-based activity that supports wider development (extrinsic)? What we have found is that where the quality of the musical experience is good (not necessarily the quality of the artistic output, but the quality of the experience), and progress can be felt and heard by participants and audience alike, all the benefits, whether intrinsic or extrinsic, are more present for those taking part.

The quality of the artistic output itself of course cannot and should not be completely disregarded. But with children and young people with varied natural ability; previous opportunities to do something musical; parental support; cultural references and backgrounds; and relative privilege or deprivation, it can be unhelpful to set firm benchmarks of what level they should be able to achieve in their singing or music-making. This is even more true where teachers are working with children with special educational needs or disabilities, either in a mixed ability group in mainstream schools or in special schools.

> **What is important is the journey. That you begin in one place, able to do certain things, and then progress to a point where you can do those things better and learn to tackle new challenges with enjoyment and a sense of achievement, rather than anxiety and pressure.**

Making it happen

For the quality of the experience to be good and for musical progress to be made, expert leadership is needed. It doesn't happen by magic! Poor leadership will give a poor experience and the benefits won't happen. The vocal leader needs first to be able to observe where improvements can be made and secondly, have strategies to make those improvements. We've pulled together some expert advice, guidance and tips in this book to help you lead singing well.

It is the artistic, expressive and creative experience of music-making and singing that make the extrinsic benefits so powerful. Music-making, and singing in particular, does something unique to our bodies and minds and it is this which we wish to harness for all children and young people to benefit their early development and for lifelong enjoyment. Let's get started!

"Singing is so central to these schools that teaching assistants, administrators, playground supervisors and parents are all happy to take on a role in fostering singing."

Sing Up Awards – A Qualitative Evaluation, 2011

"The students have gained so much from music and singing beyond just the singing itself."

Stephen Whittle, Principal, Hayes School

"Since we started our journey towards becoming a Singing School our school has been dramatically transformed from having a couple of hymn practices a week to having music embedded in nearly every daily activity in our school."

Joca Dalledone, Pope John RC Primary School

"Singing has totally transformed this school."

Catherine Andrews, class teacher, Bromley

"Singing threads through the whole life of this school and has created a positive ethos around the whole school. Our results are the result of the music that threads through the school."

Ann Golding, Head Teacher, Highfield Infants School

2

THE SINGING SCHOOL JOURNEY

To help create structure in your pursuit, we have created three levels of Singing School – Silver, Gold and Platinum. This is to help you set achievable targets related to your school's progress and so you always know where to find the next step on your journey. This chapter, along with chapters 10 and 11, focus on the criteria for achieving these levels.

Whether your journey begins here, or whether you and your school already participate in singing and you wish to enhance it, you can find a stage applicable to you. At every stage, a Singing School involves pupils, staff (teaching and non-teaching), the senior leadership team, governors and the whole school community.

Silver Singing Schools

The silver stage is the initial stage. If your journey is beginning as you read this book, these are the first things you should aim to implement in your school. In summary, Silver Singing Schools commit wholeheartedly to singing regularly, and have concrete plans in place to broaden and improve the singing already taking place and to underpinning their wider school development plans and strategies with singing.

Silver Singing Goals
For pupils

- All pupils sing more than twice a week, in and out of the music lesson.
- Pupils share singing with their peers.
- Pupils identify ways to improve their singing.
- Pupils contribute ideas to broaden singing activity in the school including choosing repertoire.

For staff

- Staff are introduced to the Singing School concept and encouraged to support the Singing School Coordinator by getting involved.
- At least two staff commit to leading singing regularly.
- Staff support the development of vocal work across the school day encouraging all children's contributions to singing.
- Staff understand the basics of good vocal health.

For the senior leadership team and governors (SLT)

- The SLT endorse the decision to work towards singing goals and ensure all members of the school know about and support the process.
- The SLT consider how singing can support the School Development Plan and wider school planning.

For the whole school community

- The whole school (or as large a group as is practically possible) sings together at least once a week.
- Families and visitors have opportunities to participate in the school's singing activities.

Gold Singing Schools

If singing is already an integral part of the school day, for pupils and staff alike, the Gold Singing Goals will help you take it to the next level. Gold Singing Schools have a breadth of singing happening for all pupils across a range of contexts throughout the school day. Singing has become a central part of the school culture and ethos and underpins wider school development plans and strategies.

Gold Singing Goals
For pupils

- Pupils sing every day in a variety of contexts.
- Pupils are supported to lead singing and vocal work.
- Pupils practise ways to improve their singing.
- Pupils sing in a range of ways and styles including creating original music with their voices.

For staff

- Staff sing weekly, including the SLT.
- Three or more staff lead singing at least twice a week and are developing confidence.
- Staff identify strategies to extend creative vocal work into the wider school day.
- Staff identify strategies to improve the quality of singing.
- Singing leaders model and share good vocal practice with colleagues.

For the senior leadership team and governors (SLT)

- The SLT are involved in the process and actively support staff and pupils to develop as singers and vocal leaders.
- The SLT demonstrate continued whole-school support and encourage further development.

For the whole school community

- Singing energises a range of everyday school activities and routines.
- Communal singing marks significant moments of school life and families and visitors share in this.

Platinum Singing Schools

We describe these schools as 'Ambassador Schools' because they extend participation in singing to the wider school community with an outward focus – inspiring and sharing their singing ethos. We will look at the Platinum framework in more detail in Chapter 11 at the end of the book.

Platinum Singing Goals

For pupils

- Pupils enjoy singing over a sustained period of time, including through passages of transition, demonstrating progress.
- Pupils show an independence and spontaneity in singing leadership both in and outside the classroom.
- Pupils develop confidence and understanding and model ways to improve their singing.
- Pupils experience a diverse range of high-quality singing opportunities in and outside the school and are supported to extend their interests.

For staff

- Staff become advocates for singing.
- All are involved in leading singing.
- Staff develop inspirational singing activity in and beyond the school through collaboration and partnership, signposting pupils to a range of opportunities.
- All staff understand the importance of good vocal health and care for the voices of those they work with.

For the senior leadership team and governors (SLT)

- The SLT champion and join in singing as a key part of school life.
- They advocate a range of approaches in using singing to benefit the school and the wider community.

For the whole school community

- Staff and pupils find routes to enjoy singing, aspire to and achieve excellence and make progress in and outside school.
- The school has opportunities to hear and participate in singing outside the school and to experience a diverse range of singing.

Platinum schools act as advocates for singing in the following ways:

- They have an outward focus, inspiring and connecting to the wider community, such as organising a singing event for local schools.
- They link with and support local schools with their progress to becoming Singing Schools.
- They link with local schools to help develop Young Singing Leaders in their area.

A vision of your school as a Singing School

This is where you think about your own school. Let's begin with some reflective questions to get you started:

1. Who are you going to need to enlist and involve in early discussions about your journey to becoming a Singing School? Who are the key decision-makers you need to speak to first? Who might be your natural allies in getting the idea off the ground to begin with?

2. What singing and music is already happening across the school? Conduct a mini-audit of what is already common practice. Get permission to visit other classrooms and areas where singing and music already happen, and document what happens, who is leading it, which pupils are involved and how often it takes place. This will give you a sense of what you have already that you can build upon and spread more widely.

Singing activity 1		Day
		Time
	Location	Frequency

Singing activity 2		Day
		Time
	Location	Frequency

Singing activity 3		Day
		Time
	Location	Frequency

Singing activity 4		Day
		Time
	Location	Frequency

Singing activity 5		Day
		Time
	Location	Frequency

3. Decide on a timeframe for achieving your goals. Make sure it is realistic and achievable but is challenging enough to be motivating and galvanise action.

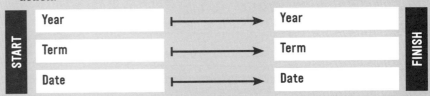

4. Who might be in a small working group with you to help with the planning?

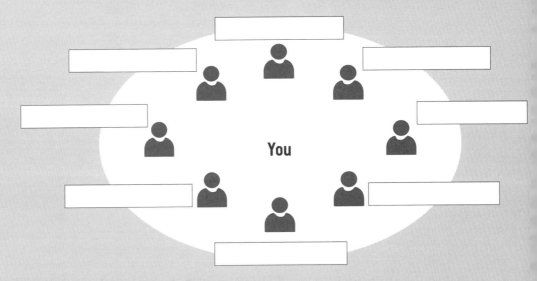

5. What barriers do you think you will encounter? For example, pressures on time or teachers' lack of confidence in singing with their pupils, or in leading singing with their class.

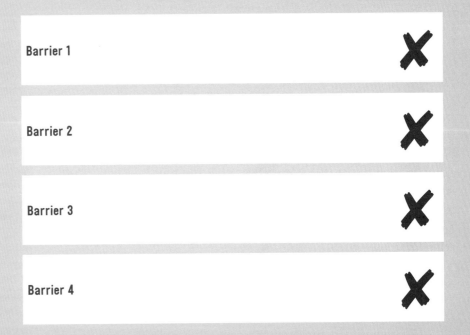

Barrier 1

Barrier 2

Barrier 3

Barrier 4

6. How will you overcome these barriers? Don't forget that vocal leaders don't necessarily need a background in music or musical training. Confidence, enthusiasm, support and good quality resources will go a long way.

Solution 1 ✔

Solution 2 ✔

Solution 3 ✔

Solution 4 ✔

7. What are the top five things becoming a Singing School will achieve for your school? Think about the school's key challenges and problems. How might singing help with pupil inclusion, behavioural issues, self-esteem, attendance and learning outcomes? How might it help foster a positive ethos and sense of community?

1.

2.

3.

4.

5.

8. What training and CPD is needed for staff in order to achieve your vision? Where might you source external help with providing this? How does this need relate to your ambitions for the vocal progress you would like pupils to make as they move up through the school?

Training	Provider	Importance (1-5)

9. Can you create some performance moments to give teachers and pupils something to work towards? When will these be and where will they happen? Have you planned in sufficient time to make sure everyone is ready? Consider local venues and organisations to partner with.

Performance 1

Audience

Location

Date / Time

Rehearsal Time

Performance 2

Audience

Location

Date / Time

Rehearsal Time

Performance 3

Audience

Location

Date / Time

Rehearsal Time

10. Finally, visualise walking through the school in 12 months' time. What singing do you hear? What is happening around the school? Who is taking part? Who is leading the singing? And what are the outcomes for the pupils? What will governors and parents be saying about the school now that it is a Singing School?

Area in the school, e.g. classroom, hall or playground	What singing is happening?	Who is taking part?	Outcome for pupils:

What are parents and governors saying?

The Singing School Coordinator

If you are reading this book, chances are that you are going to be the individual catalyst behind making your school a Singing School. You can't do the job on your own however, you will need first to persuade staff across the school to help you to build momentum and commitment to the journey you are going on. You might want to suggest to your line manager that your role in being the catalyst in this work becomes a Continuing Professional Development target for you for the coming year. You might want to suggest that a title is created for the role – something like Singing School Champion, or, as we call it, the Singing School Coordinator.

First, you will need to have obtained commitment and enthusiasm from at least the head teacher and a couple of other colleagues so you will need all the persuasive arguments about what benefits will accrue to the school and its pupils on the tip of your tongue, and backed up by compelling evidence and case studies from other schools to get them on board. Use Chapter 1 and the research references in the endnotes to help you with this.

Next, you will need to work closely with small working group you have just identified to take your planning forward, making sure that you involve the wider school community as you go.

Finally, once you are a Singing School, you are implementing your plans and the regular singing is taking place, you will need a planned process for maintaining and progressing the singing as a school and to support the progress of individual pupils.

Here are some ideas to inspire and motivate your school – staff, pupils, senior leadership team and governors and the wider school community – to work hard towards becoming a Singing School.

For your head teacher and senior leadership team

- **Explain the benefits of singing** using ideas from Chapter 1 and the endnotes.
- **Encourage the senior leadership team and governors to read Chapter 1.**
- **Create a PowerPoint presentation** of the Singing School journey you want to embark on. You can include the Singing Goals for the stage you are aiming for.
- **Meet with your head teacher** to discuss how you might embed singing activity in school planning. Support wider school goals by weaving singing into your School Development Plan.

For teaching and non-teaching staff

It's important that every member of staff is involved, so here are some ways to get them started:

- **Introduce all your colleagues to some songs.** You could host a singing staff meeting to teach a couple of songs to all your colleagues and then visit their classrooms and help them introduce the songs to their pupils. You will begin to build a small bank of songs the whole school can sing and which your colleagues have the confidence to lead on their own.

Sing Up's Song Bank is crammed full of engaging songs, or you may have other repertoire that you already use to get you going.

- **Hold a singing presentation for staff** to tell them about the importance of singing. Incorporate in your presentation a brief summary of the benefits of singing which include:

  - Development of memory
  - Improved listening skills
  - Improved language acquisition
  - Deeper understanding of rhyme and phonics
  - Development of patterning skills
  - Improvement in emotional and physical well-being
  - Involvement in aerobic activity
  - Reduction in stress and management of anger and frustration
  - A positive and safe way to address difficult issues
  - Learning to work as a team as well as valuing individuals
  - Being creative and having fun
  - Being a great stress buster for staff

- **Get the whole school involved.** For example:

  - The whole staff could consider how singing can support wider school development aims and build this into wider school planning.
  - Let the Parent Association, governors, parents and children know about the plan to become a Singing School – they may have great suggestions that will support your journey.
  - Subject/Key Stage leaders could identify songs that fit topics and add them to subject planning documents.
  - Staff with responsibility for pupils with special educational needs or disabilities could suggest ways of using singing activities to include, engage and support these pupils.
  - Staff with particular pupils who are struggling with their learning or finding their place in the school community may be able to use singing to engage with their pupils and increase their self-confidence. As their confidence grows these pupils can be given a special role (see Young Singing Leaders in Chapter 4, page 50).

- **Make singing a regular occurrence** in your school community. If singing becomes an everyday occurrence, the children and staff will overcome any initial reserve and embarrassment. Talk to the staff and pupils about the kinds of songs they like singing. Create a 'song of the week' scheme for each year group or class. Some classes like to display a sign on the classroom door or wall that says, "Our song of the week is…". The pupils can vote for their favourite.

- **Make singing resources available in the staff room.** Create a box to display useful print resources so that staff can borrow them to get ideas and tips about using singing in their classroom.

- **Encourage staff to support each other and share success stories.** This will inspire everyone to learn new ways of using songs in their classrooms and boost confidence in sharing good practice. You might want to consider creating a termly staff meeting in which to do this.

"Teaching staff have embraced singing by singing regularly, attending CPD and composing transition songs, while lunchtime supervisors are singing skipping games with children in the playground."

Catrin Jones, Shelthorpe Primary School

Download your Singing School Pledge Certificate from the product page on fabermusicstore.com and display it in school.

3

VOCAL HEALTH

To become a Singing School, teachers and pupils need to know a little about the main tool they are going to be working with – their voices. The voice is our first musical instrument, it is the instrument that everyone has, and from our earliest moments of life we are learning to use it, experimenting with the sounds it can make and using it to communicate with others.

It is a part of our bodies and so is made of the same stuff that the rest of our anatomy is made of – muscle, cartilage, tissue – and is as susceptible as other parts of our bodies to illness, stress, strain and injury. So, we need to know how to take care of it. For teachers in particular, it is a vital tool of the trade. Teachers spend a huge amount of time communicating through speaking, often when tired, stressed and sometimes straining to be heard. As a result, they are very prone to developing vocal problems.

Children's voices are still developing as their physical vocal apparatus grows and they gradually become more and more in control of it. When they are little their physical vocal apparatus is smaller and different to an adult's, so there are things an adult's voice can do which a young child's can't. If we are responsible for leading singing with children, we need to be aware of these differences and make sure that we are not encouraging them to strain their voices, and also, that we are teaching them good vocal health and technique for later life. Bad habits learnt early on are difficult to un-learn.

There isn't room here to provide a comprehensive guide to vocal health and technique but this chapter will give you the essentials and a general overview. A fuller explanation is available to Sing Up Members called 'Inside the Voice' written by vocal experts Jenevora Williams and Stuart Barr, which has informed this chapter.

Please include this slip in your envelope
Return To
Michelle James
2 The Green,
Hayes,
Bromley,
BR2 7NP
United Kingdom

Look after your own voice first

Research shows that teachers are far more likely to suffer voice problems than people in other professions. National Health Service data shows that teachers are nine times more likely to be a voice clinic patient than the average adult. And teachers of primary-aged pupils (4–11 year olds) are the most likely of all to suffer. This might be connected with average class-size, or general noise levels in a primary class, or that more of a primary teacher's time is spent speaking than with older age-groups.

Five main factors can negatively affect our vocal health:

- Using the voice for too long
- Using the voice too loudly
- Poor vocal technique
- Illness
- Emotional stress

Using the voice for too long

Instead of speaking for long periods of time, which will cause voice strain, try to build in frequent breaks.

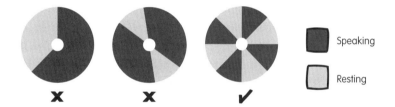

Using the voice too loudly

Whether speaking or singing, try to keep within the natural range of your voice and not strain to be too loud. Teachers can fall into the habit of using a higher-impact voice quality than is necessary. Prolonged use of this tone of voice will make your voice tired.

Instead of straining your voice in class, experiment with ways of gaining your pupils' attention – by clapping your hands for example – to give a signal that it is time for them to be quiet. Try to make a rule for yourself that you won't speak until the classroom is quiet enough for you to be heard while speaking in a normal, unstrained voice.

Poor vocal technique

We'll talk about vocal technique for your pupils later in this chapter.
For yourself, try following these simple rules:

- Don't hunch, twist or bend while using your voice. It puts the voice and your breathing apparatus under strain.
- Stand or sit up straight, with a straight back, relaxed neck and shoulders.
- Warm up your voice before you use it. Like any part of the body, your

voice needs warming-up to avoid strain. We'll look more at how to use warm-ups later on. They don't need to take long and you can do them in the shower or in the car on your way to work.

- Get to know when your voice is starting to feel tired and rest it before you suffer more serious problems.

Illness

Illnesses which affect the respiratory system – like coughs and colds – are likely to affect your voice. Try to get plenty of rest (rest your voice and get enough sleep) and drink plenty of water. Old-fashioned remedies like inhaling steam with a towel over your head actually do work. It helps to rehydrate the throat and soothe irritation. Not getting ill in the first place is the best solution.

Other health-related suggestions if you are having problems with your voice:

- Keep a bottle of water with you and take frequent sips through the day.
- Avoid caffeinated drinks and alcohol.
- Try to avoid eating just before going to bed. It can cause acid reflux which can irritate the throat and voice.
- Don't smoke.

Emotional stress

Your voice is particularly vulnerable to stress. In extreme cases, prolonged periods of emotional stress have been known to cause people to lose their voice entirely or to lose part of their vocal range. Tension manifests itself very readily in the physical apparatus we use to speak and sing; it can cause the throat, chest and shoulders to tense-up and this can put the voice under significant strain. Think about how hard it is to try to sing when you are crying, or how your voice wobbles when you are upset or angry.

Breathing exercises are a good way to reduce stress. You are more likely to get ill or use your voice less effectively if you are stressed or worried.

Warm-ups

Warming up the voice before use can prevent injury, improve technique, help with motion, eliminate tension and make our brains more alert.

A good vocal warm-up should:

- Warm up vocal muscles and the brain
- Release tension
- Work on ease and range of motion in the muscles
- Do small work before big work.

A vocal warm-up routine should involve:

- Waking up and balancing the body
- Attention to breathing
- Releasing the head, neck and throat
- Warming up the larynx

- Exploring resonance
- Clarifying articulation

Common misconceptions

Warming up involves lots of jumping up and down. This might be fun and get your pupils energised but since you don't use your legs much for singing it won't be of direct benefit.

Warming up is a luxury I don't have time for. It really needn't take long – five minutes or less – and it will mean you get more out of the singing when you get to it.

Warming up your speaking voice

It's a really good idea to warm up your voice before everyday use if you are a teacher and it only needs to take two or three minutes. Here's what you can do:

- **Body stretch**: Stretch your arms up then gently flop forwards from the waist, letting your arms dangle. Have a little shake to release tension. Slowly roll yourself back to an upright position until your back is straight and you imagine your head is being pulled gently upwards by a piece of string. This will align your back and neck nicely.
- **Released breathing**: Do some slow hisses with your hand on your belly button. Feel your stomach pull in. Then release your stomach muscles as you breathe in again.
- **Range**: On a humming sound or an 'ng' sound, slide up and down like a siren. Gradually go a little higher and a little lower to reach the more extreme ends of your voice range.
- **Efficient voicing**: Siren up and down to some buzzes ('vvv' and 'zzz') making sure they sound buzzy and not breathy. Think of using very little air in your sound. Then siren up and down to open vowel sounds.

Posture

Standing up straight with the ear, shoulder, hip, knee and foot in alignment, without locking the knees, is what we are aiming for. For longer singing sessions where some periods of being seated are necessary, sitting on the front of a chair with a straight back is okay. Sitting on the floor should be avoided if possible. Primary-school children do spend quite a lot of time sitting on the floor, but it isn't the best position for good healthy singing because all their respiratory equipment will be scrunched up. If you think about the warm-up exercises described in this chapter – the stretching and releasing of tension – you will see that it is impossible to replicate those body positions while sitting on the floor.

Tip ▶ **Soldier, Teenager, Singer**

Encourage good posture and breathing from the start. 'Soldier, Teenager, Singer' is a great exercise for this. Call out 'soldier' and the children must stand to attention, shout 'teenager' and they mime a slouching teen, call out 'singer' and they stand straight with balanced head and soft knees.

Registers

One goal of singing training is to iron out gaps between registers. Registers are often referred to as 'chest' and 'head' voices, terminology which reveals the historic (but inaccurate) idea of different places of resonance for different registers. Research has revealed that the registers are actually created by differing vocal fold vibration patterns rather than places of resonance.

Singers who have not yet learned to blend registers experience a noticeable change from the thicker, 'chest' voice to the thinner, 'head' voice. The head voice is often the weaker register, but can be improved with work on resonance, breathiness and through general familiarity.

Blurring the distinction between registers can be achieved by sliding up and down to 'ng' (as in 'sing'). This helps the singer work out their mechanism for getting from one register to the other. Once this has been mastered, use open vowel sounds. Then try using scales that cross the register breaks, keeping the same smoothness of sound found on the slide.

Good vocal technique

Understanding the basics of good vocal technique and helping your pupils to adopt them is part of the responsibility of being a singing leader. Good technique will produce a better sound and will help protect the voice against wear and tear. It will also stand pupils in good stead for later in life if they want to continue with singing. Inappropriate habits can set in if the young singer imitates the sound made by adults with much more advanced technique.

With a good vocal technique, what you are trying to achieve is efficiency of voicing – most sound for minimal effort and fine muscle control – using only the muscles that are needed.

Tip ▶ **Singers are athletes**

When you are warming-up with your pupils, make the connection between warming up to sing and warming up before physical exercise. You could show them video footage of Olympic athletes or a football team doing their warm-ups before a match. Explain to them that because they are using their bodies when they sing, they need to warm them up first to be able to sing well.

Warm-up 1: Wake up and balance the body

- Gently work torso muscles by jogging on the spot, circling your arms, or dancing.
- Stretch the torso muscles with some forward bending and side stretches. Keep breathing normally while stretching.
- Release tension in the neck, shoulders and jaw with yawning, gentle neck stretches, shoulder circling (forwards and backwards) and shoulder scrunches. Do circles with the head – down to the chest, round to the shoulder and back again (not tilting the head backwards). Small, gentle movements are just as effective as big ones.
- Stand straight, but in a natural position with the weight evenly balanced between toes and heels and from side to side, without stiff knees. It is much easier to breathe when your posture is straight.

Warm-up 2: Breathing

The aim here is to be making use of the lower abdomen (stomach) for breathing rather than shoulders and upper chest, but without undue effort. It should feel natural and unforced.

- Get your singers to put their hands on their bellies to feel the movement in as they sing, and out as they breathe in.
- Use 'shhh', 'fff' or 'sss' sounds to feel this movement initially and then voiced sounds 'vvv' and 'zzz'. You can also try a rolled 'rrr' and 'brrr'.
- Now try this to rhythmic patterns of hisses or shushes and feel the flexibility of the muscles.

Warm-up 3: Release the throat

When we sing, we want to avoid the throat being constricted because this causes tension and affects the sound we produce. We are aiming to sing with an 'open throat'. Try these exercises to get the feel of it:

- Breathe in as silently as possible and as if you have just had a happy surprise – imagine you've won the lottery or been given a great present.
- Imagine a silent giggle in your throat. Practise returning to a natural throat position and then the silent giggle position.
- Try imitating monkey noises – 'ooh ooh ooh aah aah aah' – with a feeling of looseness in the throat.
- Sing through closed but vibrating lips, with puffy cheeks. The muscles of the face and lips should be soft, and the sound should be gentle.

Warm-up 4: The voice

This is actually an exercise to warm up what are known as the 'vocal folds'. The aim is to exercise the voice throughout the pitch range and to practise clear tone and 'onsets' – how you start a sung note – and also iron-out register breaks – where the voice shifts from one place to another and there can be an audible 'gap'.

- Slide up and down small distances (across no more than the distance of five notes apart) to 'ng'. Gradually expand the range of the slide to higher and lower pitches.
- Think of using as little air as possible in the sound, while keeping the sound clear and mobile.
- Extend the pitch range to include both extremes of the voice.
- Open from 'ng' onto quiet vowel sounds: 'ee' – 'eh' – 'ah' – 'oh' – 'oo'.
- Do the same sliding exercises using 'vvv' and 'zzz'. Then try sliding on a rolled 'rrr' and 'brrr.'
- Try singing 'heeh' with a breathy 'h' at the start. This should give a very gentle start to the note. Then practise singing 'uh-oh,' which will have a bumpy start to the note. Finally sing 'eee' with no breathiness or bump at the beginning of the note, just a nice clean start.

Warm-up 5: Explore resonance

Practising how well your voice resonates helps build voice projection and means you don't have to try so hard to sing loudly, which can put strain on the voice.

- Have fun making witch-like cackle noises and quacking – this will be a very nasal sound.
- Then try this sensation with the resonance in the mouth and not the nose.
- Try whooping and calling sounds, using the upper register. Using the sounds we make for spontaneous emotional expression will often be the most efficient.

Warm-up 6: Clarify articulation

These exercises help with the singing of text:

- Drop the jaw like a trap door, without letting it move forward. Sing 'ya ya ya' exercises with the tongue doing the articulation and the jaw loose but still.
- Practise tongue isolation by touching the outer edge of the upper and lower lips with the tip of the tongue, without moving the jaw forward.
- Put a finger between your lightly closed teeth and sing a phrase. Then drop your jaw, let your tongue hang out and do the same.
- Check that the tongue does not press back as it moves towards 'ah'. There should still be a feeling of lift in the middle. As you move from 'ah' through 'oh' to 'oo', the change will primarily come from bringing the lips forward, with minimal tongue movement.
- Once you've practised these articulations, use your own tongue-twisters sung on descending scales.

Developing voices and voice change

The way the voice changes through puberty is a sensitive issue, particularly for boys, who will be acutely aware of the audible vocal shift. For young people with some competence in singing, interest may wane as they try to navigate a changing voice. Those with a more developed singing competency can be demoralised by a temporarily shortened range and unpredictable sound.

It's easy to make assumptions about why boys in particular lose interest in singing. Singing is commonly cited as being 'girly', with insufficient male role models or 'cool' repertoire to excite boys. While these issues may well play a part, there are other physical reasons why young people, girls too, shy away from singing around the age of puberty. Sensitive and skilled singing leaders can ensure that this age-group are guided appropriately on their singing journey, giving them the chance they deserve to take their singing further.

These are the principal characteristics of voice change:

- A deepening of the speaking voice and lowering of the singing *tessitura* (comfortable range)
- A contraction of the range
- A loss of vocal agility
- Difficulty with lift points or *passagio* (transition between registers)
- Hoarseness, missing notes and a tendency to 'crack' in boys
- Breathiness and missing notes in girls

Changing anatomy[7]

It's crucial that singing leaders get clued up on a number of key points in order to guide young singers, starting with the fact that most boys experience voice change somewhere between the ages of 11 and 14, at different times for each individual. This occurs because of a rapid maturation and growth of the larynx and vocal tract, triggered by the same endocrinal changes that stimulate sexual maturation. The thyroid cartilage stretches from being rounded to an elliptical shape, and there is a lengthening and thickening of the vocal folds (sometimes called vocal cords). These are the membranous muscle tissue layers that vibrate and modulate airflow to create sound.

When the elongating vocal folds snap together and peel apart to modulate air from the lungs, the pitch becomes deeper. This is often accompanied by a marked facial change in boys: bones grow, creating larger cavities in the sinuses, nose and throat for the voice to resonate in. All this means that during the short period of maturation, the male voice can descend by a whole octave.

When vocal change typically becomes more noticeable, the commonly used phrase 'his voice is starting to break' comes into use – a phrase that can be quite unhelpful, suggesting that there is something wrong. This can be a catastrophic notion to a keen young singer, so speaking of 'voice change' more accurately describes what is in fact a natural process.

The voice can become somewhat unpredictable during this phase, with the *tessitura* narrowing to around a fifth or a sixth. Boys will still want to sound good, so if your young singers are struggling to sing well, look at the range of the material.

We can think of boys' voices in 3 stages:

1. Unchanged
2. Changing (or Cambiata)[8]
3. Changed

In girls, typical symptoms of voice change are breathy tone, contracting range, shifting *tessitura* and the appearance of breaks between different parts of the voice. Experts recommend against classifying girls as soprano or contralto at this age, when they need reassurance that their vocal limitations are due to voice change and are therefore temporary.[9]

For both males and females, understanding what's going on with their voice will help them stick with it through this period of transition.

Meanwhile, teachers should be aware that the year immediately prior to voice change (around age 10–11) can be a 'golden year' for singing, with boys' and girls' voices blending well in unison. In an ideal world, all boys would have learned to sing to a reasonable standard at primary school and the specialist music teacher working with 11-year-olds should enjoy bringing what has been learned to a final state of perfection before voice change seriously begins. This is the golden singing year and the vocal foundation of the best musical learning that is to come.

An initial sort-out

Here's a fun way of finding out what you've got in a new class. Have everybody stand and keep singing *Oh when the saints* in the key of D major (note: the range is a fifth). If you have any boys completing change, they will automatically sing it an octave below. Whiz round the class to identify them and indicate for them to sit down and stop singing. Now, with the remainder still standing, transpose up a fourth to G major – more will drop an octave. You have found the cambiata boys who can now also sit down. If done with boys on their own, you may well be left with some still standing who are unchanged trebles. In a mixed-gender class, though, it may be only the girls left standing. It's probably best to accept this, as boys may not want to be identified as the ones who 'sing like girls'.

Finding an individual's range

During voice change, the lowest sung note will usually be about two or three semitones below the average pitch of the speaking voice. A common way of finding this is to ask the student to count slowly backwards from twenty and find the note on a keyboard that most closely matches the pitch you hear. Then go down three semitones and you will have the lowest possible singing note. If you go up a sixth from the speaking note, you will have the highest note that can comfortably be sung. Some students will be able to go higher, but none lower. It's not a good idea to go higher for too long. Most importantly of all, just keep everyone singing throughout the voice change process, there's absolutely no reason to stop.

| Tip | Top Tips on developing voices |

1. Avoid having a lift point in the middle of the song, forcing boys to move between modal (natural) range and falsetto. Move into falsetto only for the climax of the song.

2. Don't keep boys at the top of their modal range without crossing into falsetto. This will result in strain, fatigue and a poor sound, contributing to the belief that 'boys can't sing.'

3. Don't exceed the range of a sixth until the voice has settled down.

4. Be mindful of choral and traditional folk repertoire that may have too great a range for adolescent voices. The period of change might be a good time to explore pop songs which often don't exceed a sixth.

5. If there are problems negotiating intervals, it might be that the tessitura isn't right. Bear in mind that vocal folds might not be able to change their shape and vibratory pattern quickly enough to pitch some intervals.

6. When some of the class haven't experienced voice change but others have, the latter can be invited to sing down the octave – or invited to choose which octave to sing.

7. Be mindful later on, when more pupils have experienced voice change than haven't, that the remainder might try to sing down the octave before they are ready. A good range to try is D to A just below middle C. This won't go too low for boys approaching baritone, and later maturing boys and girls can sing up the octave (D to A just above middle C).

8. Sing gently. Never demand loud singing.

9. Use mainly the new notes that appear at the bottom of the voice.

10. Treat every student as an individual and differentiate accordingly. You cannot go by year group or chronological age.

VOCAL LEADERSHIP

What do we mean by vocal leadership? Just standing at the front smiling encouragingly? Conducting? Somewhere in the middle? What makes it effective? Why bother doing it?

In this chapter, we will look at vocal leadership and the extent to which how you lead singing affects:

- Pupil engagement
- The creation of a supportive environment
- Pupil inclusion
- The progress pupils make
- Communication and understanding
- Creativity
- Your own learning and that of your pupils
- Musical learning specifically
- Community building
- Voice care

We will also think about the range of contexts there are for singing in schools and the implication this has on the style of singing leading you choose to use, whether that be starting off a routine song or leading a singing practice and choir performance.

There is a place for all types of singing in school from the informal sing-along on the school bus to the more formal school concert and everything in between. All will benefit from some type of leadership whether that be literally starting to sing and encouraging others to join in through to conducting the choir and instrumental accompaniment.

By providing some direction, you can help your pupils to sing as an ensemble, begin at the same time, on the same note, with the same pulse and communicate the music to a listener.

Leading singing will help your singers to:

- Understand the music
- Achieve ensemble skills
- Listen well
- Give a more effective performance.

As a leader of singing you can:

- Keep the singers together
- Indicate the dynamics and expression
- Illustrate the shape of the melody
- Provide a visual aide memoire as to what comes next in the song
- Provide some 'scaffolding' for your singers – for pitch and melody, rhythm and pulse, words and meaning, actions, tone and technique, singing loudly and softly, phrasing.

But not everybody needs to be able to 'conduct' formally. You can start from an understanding of how what you do can support and help your young singers to do better when they sing and gradually build out from there.

Contexts for vocal leadership

Let's think about the many different types and contexts of vocal leadership that might occur in school. Here is a list of some of them:

- Formal choir conducting
- A singing assembly
- A singing practice
- Singing in a class music lesson
- Singing in the classroom as an aid to learning
- Singing routine songs – singing the register, singing a goodbye song
- Playground singing games
- A religious service, or collective worship
- Nursery rhyme singing with pre-school children

Use this space to think about and write down the different types of singing that are happening currently in your school, and who leads them:

Next, use this space to think about and write down the different types of singing you would like to be happening in your school once you are a Singing School, and who you would like to be able to lead them. Don't worry if not all these people already have the skills and confidence to lead the singing, this is what you are going to work towards achieving:

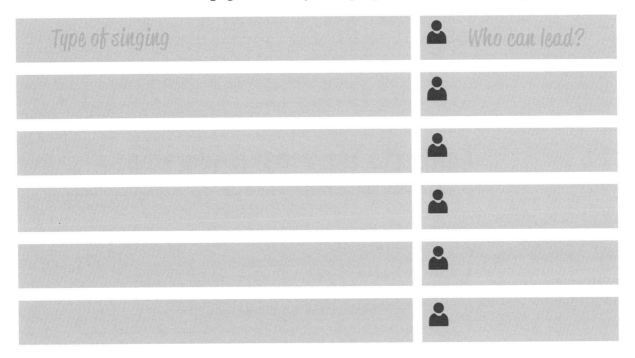

Types of leading in different contexts

As you can probably see from your list, there are different types of singing that you have in your vision for your Singing School, and these will require varying degrees of expertise from the individuals who lead them.

The kind of leadership techniques needed to lead singing in different contexts often depend on the practicalities of the contexts themselves. These will be considerations like:

- Space in which the singing is happening – is it large or small?
- Will it be easy or difficult for everyone to hear each other well?
- Number of singers – is it a large group or a small group?
- What is the purpose of the singing – for learning outcomes, for routine building/behaviour, for performance, for fun, for community-building?
- Will there be an audience? How formal is the occasion?
- How complex or easy is the material you are going to sing?

Consider for a moment, a completely different context – a football stadium. With upwards of 25,000 fans across more than 130 metres singing leadership is most certainly needed. This takes the form of a self-nominated singing section, within which is at least one individual singing leader who stands, often with their back to the football pitch and leads the singing. They do this with a combination of – you guessed it – confidence and enthusiasm. Plus, a loud voice, lots of clapping of the pulse and a buddy with a drum. The songs are learnt through repetition over a period of time – many of the songs are passed down across generations of fans. It is a great example of how singing is an important element of building a community and being part of a collective. There is an expectation that singing will happen, it is a natural element of the event, so most people sing.

The orchestral conductor[10]

Let's begin at one end of the spectrum, let's think about the role of an orchestral conductor and then we will look at what we, as singing leaders in school, can learn from how the conductor does their job.

What is the role of the conductor of an orchestra? All the members of that orchestra are already expert musicians, top class performers, and technically excellent at playing their instrument. They have the music in front of them and know exactly what they are supposed to be playing and when. No-one needs to help them with technique, no-one needs to teach them the piece of music, no-one needs to explain to them the conventions of playing in a symphony orchestra. So, what can a conductor possibly add that they couldn't manage on their own? What are the reasons why orchestras need and benefit from having a conductor?

To keep time

The first role of a conductor is to beat time. In the 19th century, as western classical composers wrote for bigger and bigger orchestras, it became more and more difficult for everyone to hear each other. The previous convention of either the harpsichord player or the principal violin player leading the whole group, no longer worked. The physical distance between that player and the players at the extreme edges of the group became too large for either a visual or aural connection to be maintained between them.

Then there's the time it takes for sound to travel – think thunder and lightning – we know that sound travels more slowly than light. This means that in a big orchestra, if you are sitting at the back playing the timpani, by the time you've heard the line from the first violins, you are already late. So, you are dependent on the visual cue from the conductor to keep together with the rest of the orchestra.

However, an orchestral conductor doesn't simply beat a steady pulse like a metronome; they aren't simply a visual click-track to play along to. The other convention that became more prevalent in the 19th century was for composers to write music where they intended the pulse to be 'pulled around' rather than be metronomic – known as 'rubato'. Sometimes these alterations to the pulse are written in the music, but often it is a 'feel', a shaping of the phrase or a slight pause before moving on – in other words, a subjective interpretation of meaning in the musical phrase, like an actor interpreting their lines with particular emphasis or stress on some words and deciding when to pause. Any individual musician in the orchestra will have their own slight variation on how they would personally interpret the music, but an orchestra needs to perform just one interpretation, and that is the conductor's. Actually, any individual musician in the orchestra might have a different view about the tempo, but there can only be one of those too. Again, the conductor's role in choosing and indicating the tempo is crucial, and significantly affects the character of the music.

Setting the tempo begins by having the beat firmly in your head before you make your first gesture, and then conveying that tempo to the orchestra plus indicating the precise moment when they are expected to begin playing. An orchestral conductor will normally convey all of that through just one gesture – the up-beat, but in the context of leading singing in school a verbal count-in is often fine, unless you are using a backing track. Just remember that the information you need to convey is the equivalent of the orchestral conductor's upbeat.

To provide interpretation and meaning

If the job of a conductor's right hand is to set tempo and keep time, the job of their left hand is more about conveying meaning. Each conductor will have their own style and convention for doing this. The gestures of their left hand might shape a musical phrase, indicate a line or element that they want the orchestra to listen to and be aware of, and define the character and meaning of the music being played. This is all subjective and individual but it is an important part of the conductor's role. The conductor will also bring in musicians with the left hand – this is a helpful reminder (in case they have miscounted their bars' rest!) and gives the musician a sense of how the conductor wants them to play their phrase when they do come in.

The other aspect of providing interpretation is the responsibility owed to the composer. Making sure the orchestra play what is written is one thing but to get to the heart of the intentions of the composer and to get the orchestra to play with a particular colour to their tone, or to convey a particular mood or emotion is quite another. The composer doesn't give instructions for how to do that, so it requires imagination from the conductor and the ability to hear the sound they want in their head first, and then to create the gestures to elicit that sound from the orchestra.

To listen and set balance

The conductor stands in a good position to be able to hear the overall sound as it will reach the audience. Sometimes in rehearsals conductors will wander to the back of the concert hall while the orchestra is playing to check that the sound and balance are still as they want them to be from that part of the hall.

Each individual musician in the orchestra will only be hearing their own slice of the overall sound. They will mainly be listening to themselves – making sure they are playing in tune, with the right tone and attack – and listening to those closest around them so they are contributing to the ensemble of their section appropriately. It is the conductor's job to put all the sound ingredients from the entire orchestra together to form a cohesive whole, making sure that no element is drowned out by another and that the important elements at any given moment can be heard by the audience.

It's also worth remembering that each individual musician is only looking at their part in the notation they have in front of them. The conductor has the whole score with every part in it. Score-reading is a crucial skill for the orchestral conductor and requires a lot of preparation in advance of the first rehearsal to be familiar with every corner of it so that they can lead everyone else. The conductor is the only person who knows exactly what everyone is meant to be doing at all times. Everyone else is just focussed on their own responsibilities.

To lead the orchestra and the audience

The conductor sets the tempo, phrasing, interpretation and character of the performance for the musicians to follow but their gestures also fulfil another purpose, that of leading how the audience listens to the music. The gestures the conductor uses are often technical yet also universal in their ability to convey meaning and emotion. The audience, seeing these will instinctively have their ears tuned into the same phrases and nuances that the orchestra is being directed to play, and this will greatly enhance their experience of hearing the performance. In essence, what the conductor is paying attention to, the orchestra and the audience will also pay attention to – this is their leadership role. The conductor is part director, part performer, and they use their bodies and gestures to fulfil both roles. They also use their faces, which the orchestra get to see but the audience usually don't unless the concert hall has seats behind the orchestra – which some do – and some people prefer to sit there for precisely this reason, because they get more from the experience by being able to see what the players see when they look at the conductor's facial expressions. The best conductors are quite mesmerising to watch, your eyes are drawn to them but rather than being a distraction from the performance they are quite the opposite, they are a conduit to understanding the meaning being conveyed by the music.

To be the figurehead

Like any leadership position, as well as celebrating triumphs, this can also mean being the spokesperson or advocate for the work of the orchestra. The conductor will usually be the main motivator behind the artistic vision for the ensemble and the wider organisation that supports it and leading the way 'through the hard times and the good'. The conductor will often be required to meet with or host major benefactors or donors to the orchestra, be interviewed by the media, give pre-concert talks and generally be the face of the whole organisation.

The conductor will set the tone of the culture within the orchestra – good or bad – and be the primary rule-maker/rule-enforcer about what behaviour and professional attitude is expected in rehearsals, between colleagues, in relation to work-ethic, inter-personal respect and other professional expectations.

The school singing leader

So, what can we learn from the example of the orchestral conductor that might help us to define the role of a singing leader in a school context? Quite a lot, in fact. Do you need to be a trained conductor to be a singing leader? No, but here is what we can learn from the comparison.

Teaching and learning

As a teacher, you already know how to do this which is good, because it is the main difference between your role as a school vocal leader and the role of an orchestral conductor. Unlike the orchestral conductor, you will need to teach your pupils the songs you are going to sing, and help them to learn to use the instrument in question – their voices. Later in the chapter, we will look at some techniques and approaches to help you do this. And in chapters 7, 8 and 9 we will look at:

- Singing to develop musical learning (Chapter 7)
- Starting and developing choirs (Chapter 8)
- Making progress and improving singing (Chapter 9)

Keeping time

As a vocal leader, one of your responsibilities is to make sure the singers know when and how to begin singing, and to keep them together once they have started. You might be singing with a piano accompaniment, with a backing track or unaccompanied (*a cappella*) and you'll need to do different things to achieve a clean start and keeping together in each of those contexts.

Singing with a piano or instrumental accompaniment

When singing with a piano or other instrumental accompaniment, you need to be able to communicate the pulse to the instrumentalists as well as the singers. If there is an introduction before the singers come in, you could leave the initial tempo to them as long as you have agreed what it is beforehand, and you are confident that they can set the tempo on their own. If your piano accompanist or instrumentalists are pupils, it might be safer to set the tempo yourself, particularly for a performance. It is quite common for young or inexperienced performers to rush when they are nervous.

Ensuring that the instrumentalists and singers can hear each other will help keep the ensemble together but you may need to keep reminding them to listen to each other – this will also help your singers with tuning.

Singing with a backing track

Backing tracks can be useful. If they are arranged, performed and produced well, they allow your young singers to experience singing with something of a totally professional standard in a variety of styles, which would be impossible to replicate with live performers in most schools. Using them can present some difficulties in relation to keeping everyone together and your role in this is different to when you are working only with live performers because you have no control over what the backing track does other than when it starts, when it stops and how loud it is. So, the golden rule is to make sure that you really are in control of those things.

- **When it starts**: Backing tracks usually have an introduction so you need to make sure that you and your singers are really familiar with the introduction and know what their cue is to come in. You might want to encourage them to know how many bars long it is, and teach them how to count these silently in their heads. Or you might prefer to simply get them very used to hearing it and practising when to come in.
- **When it stops**: Familiarise yourselves with the ending, particularly if there is any slowing down or pause at the end and practise singing in time with the backing track. Do lots of listening to the backing track first and preferably, if it is a Sing Up track, listen to the performance track too, so you can hear how our singers sing the ending.
- **How loud it is**: This is possibly the most important thing to control. Performances can go really wrong if the singers can't hear the backing track. Tempo and pitching can drift dramatically and this can feel really destabilising for the singers and the audience. Make sure that the sound system you are using is up to the job and can play the track loudly enough without distortion to be easy to hear comfortably and sound really good. Conversely, it is also important not to have the track so loud that the singers are tempted to strain their voices to be heard over it. You might want to stand in a few different places in the room – in with the singers while singing, at the back of the room for the audience – to check that the volume is set at the right level for everyone. Also, check with your singers that they can hear it OK, it will remind them that they are supposed to be listening to it while they're singing.

Singing *a cappella*

With smaller *a cappella* groups you might not need a leader actually conducting at the front at all. A well-rehearsed *a cappella* group will be able to lead and manage themselves with one of them taking responsibility for gesturing beginnings, endings and tempo changes from within the group.

With larger groups of more than 12 or 15 singers, it may become necessary to have a leader at the front, particularly with younger or inexperienced singers. Just for encouragement or as an aide memoire, you can be providing useful visual 'scaffolding' for them to be able to sing well and remember what you have rehearsed.

Obviously, with *a cappella* singing, you are completely in control of tempo, phrasing, dynamics etc. without needing to worry about instrumentalists or backing tracks, so there's a great opportunity for some beautifully phrased, really expressive singing. You will however need to help younger or less experienced singers to stay in tune if they are singing unaccompanied – retaining a sense of the key you are in without any firm reference point is tricky at first but can be learnt with practise. You may need to be their ears to keep them on the right path while they are learning. We'll look at techniques to improve pitch and singing in tune in Chapter 9.

> **Tip** ⟩ **One, two and off we go...**
>
> Here's a really good way of getting your singers to start on the right pitch at the same time and in the correct tempo.
>
> Find the starting note – use pitch pipes or a piano for accuracy – and clearly on that starting note, sing "One, two and off we go..." (or similar) in the tempo of the song you are about to sing.
>
> If you practise this approach regularly with your singers it will become second nature to them and it will avoid them drifting in at different times and different pitches.

Providing interpretation and meaning

In a school singing context, the vocal leader's role in relation to interpretation and meaning is two-fold.

- The first part is to help the children to think about the words they are singing and what they mean. There are lots of songs in the Song Bank which are about values – like friendship or courage – or are intended to be thought-provoking. Encourage your singers to think about, and discuss, the lyrics of the song they are singing and what they think they mean. In a school context you may also want to do some extension work around these themes in class, using the song as a starting point for wider exploration and discussion of the topics that the lyrics touch on.
- The second part is to explore how the way in which they sing the song can express and enhance the meaning of the words. Explain to your singers that singing is a musical performance and that as such, their job is to try to convey meaning to listeners – not just through the words themselves but also through how they sing each phrase. This is where your leadership comes in, because just like with an orchestra, there will be many different possible interpretations of how to sing a phrase to convey the meaning and you need to get your singers to all sing the same way as an ensemble. With some songs, you might want to work with the singers to create some actions which help to express the meaning of the song. You might want to give leading the actions as a job to a small group of your singers.

Listening and setting balance

Your role here is as much about modelling good listening as actually doing it. An essential skill for your young singers to develop is the ability to listen to each other when they are singing. By listening well yourself and commenting frequently on what you can hear you will be encouraging the singers to do the same – you should ask them what they can hear, and ask them for their comments on it.

- Do they think the singing could be improved on?
- If so, how?
- What can they hear?
- If they are singing in parts can they hear both/all the parts? Are they well balanced?
- Do they think that the words can be heard clearly?
- Do they think that they are singing together well as an ensemble?
- Are they making a good sound?
- Did they get quieter in the place where you asked them to?

In this way, you will be helping them to become good critical listeners which will really help them to improve over time.

Leading the singers and the audience

If you are the singing leader in a school performance situation you have a responsibility to lead the singing as well as the audience. Imagine you have a performance – an end of term concert or a special assembly – to which parents are invited, and that you are leading the singing. First of all, you are the 'buffer' between the audience and the performers. You need to manage the behaviour and expectations of both groups for the event to be a success. This might involve setting some gentle ground rules at the beginning.

With the choir, these rules might include:

- No talking
- Look at teacher/vocal leader
- Smile
- When to sit, when to stand
- Not to fidget or lose concentration
- How to walk on and off in an organised way

With the audience, rules might include:

- Be extra encouraging
- Join in with the singing when instructed
- Quietly remove younger siblings if they become noisy or upset

You may also want to provide some background context for the audience, for example, you might explain if learning the songs has been part of a wider project, e.g. 'we've been learning songs about our planet as part of our school-wide project about the environment and nature this term'. Or, you might want to explain what the parents should appreciate about the performance, e.g. 'we've been learning to sing in parts for the first time this term and the children have done really well to learn this song – listen out for the harmonies in the second chorus'.

Being the figurehead

Like the orchestral conductor, you will be able to celebrate the highlights of the process and outcomes of leading your school to become a Singing School. These highlights might include when the child who is very shy and has struggled to settle into school life finds their singing voice and it really boosts his or her confidence. It may be your job to shine a spotlight on these moments too, so that colleagues and the senior leadership team and governors understand and appreciate the achievements along the way. You will need to have unflagging enthusiasm for the work and motivate everyone else to come with you on the journey. And, like the orchestral conductor you will set the direction of travel, the culture and tone of the singing work, and the work-ethic of teachers and pupils alike in meeting your goals.

My school's singing contexts

Use the space here now to think about your school's different singing contexts (your aspirational ones from the previous list on page 21). Thinking about what we've learnt already about leadership in different contexts, make some judgements about what you think the appropriate form of vocal leadership might be for each of your contexts.

Reminder: The contextual factors will be things like:

- Space in which the singing is happening – is it large or small?
- Will it be easy or difficult for everyone to hear each other well?
- Number of singers – is it a large group or a small group?
- What is the purpose of the singing – for learning outcomes, for routine building/behaviour, for performance, for fun, for community-building?
- Will there be an audience? How formal is the occasion?
- How complex or easy is the material you are going to sing?

Appropriate style of leadership might include:

- Formal conducting
- Semi-formal vocal leadership – counting in, giving starting pitch, beating the pulse, keeping the pulse steady, shaping the phrases, reminder of actions/words
- Informal vocal leadership – counting in, giving starting note, singing along and leading key moments & the ending
- Self-led by singing group
- Sing-along – start singing, others join in
- Playground style – young leaders start singing as part of a game

Type of singing

Other considerations

Number of pupils

Room

Leadership style:

Equipment and staff

Type of singing

Other considerations

Number of pupils

Room

Leadership style

Equipment and staff

Type of singing:

Other considerations:

Number of pupils

Room

Leadership style

Equipment and staff

Type of singing

Other considerations

Number of pupils

Room

Leadership style

Equipment and staff

Type of singing

Other considerations

Number of pupils

Room

Leadership style

Equipment needed

Type of singing

Other considerations

Number of pupils

Room

Leadership style

Equipment and staff

Approaches to teaching a song

As with any teaching, to be effective you will:

- Match the 'work' and learning outcomes to build on pupils' skills, understanding and experience
- Know the subject matter and prepare how to teach it, anticipating where the obstacles might be
- Have considered a range of other factors such as space, resource and classroom management.

The same is true with teaching warm-ups and songs. As you experiment with the many techniques you'll start to get a feel for which methods to use with the groups you work with and with different types of song.

Knowing the music

First and foremost, knowing the music well is the first step to being able to teach a song and help pupils understand what they are singing. Here are the things to look out for in preparation for teaching a song:

- **Key and range:** Is it suitable for the voices you are working with? If there are passages where the voice would be particularly high or low then you should think about how you'll prepare the voices to cope with it through a suitable warm-up.
- **Structure:** What is the song's structure? Are there repeating sections or phrases that would be useful to teach early on? Can you remember which section follows which? How does it start and end? Most importantly, how do you get from one section to another?
- **Lyrics:** Think about what the lyrics mean and how you could convey the poetry through the expression and communication of the words using dynamics, diction and tone. If there are lots of verses, how will you help pupils remember what comes next?
- **Melody and harmony:** Do you know where and how the melody and any harmonies fit together? Do you know the starting notes of each section and part? Can you anticipate which bits might need more work than others?
- **Tricky corners:** Twists and turns in the melody, descending melodies, large leaps and very small steps in the melody can mean pupils lose their pitch and intonation so it's worth spotting these and making a feature of them in the warm-up or finding a way to describe how to navigate them when you get there. Rhythms can also sometimes cause problems: fast-moving music tends to speed up and syncopated rhythms can derail the pulse. Be prepared to work on pulse and rhythm where you see this might be an issue.
- **Style:** Think about how you'll achieve a sense of style. Is it through bending or sliding notes as in soul, R&B and blues? What about the diction in pop and rock? Should the sound be clean as in classical music? Will you be swinging the rhythm? Or maybe there are opportunities to add decoration, or characterisation as in musical theatre.

Catching a song

The expression 'catching a song' refers to children learning a song without having been consciously taught it.

TRY THIS

Pupils: aged 9–11

Touch your head, shoulder, elbows, hips, knees, toes. Next, play (or sing) the song *Baby 1, 2, 3* asking pupils to only join in with the actions. Play the track again and this time ask pupils to sing along. How much did they remember? It's highly likely that they can sing back most or all of the song. The impact of asking children to focus on the actions has meant they have had to listen closely to the words (and therefore the tune) and joining in with the actions have helped the pupils understand the phrasing and structure of the whole song, learn the words (the rhythm) and learn the shape of the melody.

Catching a song works with much younger children too, just think of all the children's songs that parents sing with their babies and toddlers that combine funny words, anticipated tickles, and actions. With younger children, you would pick simpler material with fewer words, that are easy to join in with.

The 'catching' technique also works in the following ways:

- Regular exposure to hearing a song in the background of the classroom often results in pupils catching the 'hooks' in a song such as the chorus.
- Playing a game along to the song, i.e. using stretchy lycra to bounce to the pulse, balls to roll, bounce and catch, scarves to wave, bean bags to pass, clapping games, skipping games etc.
- Listening activities connected with the story of a song.

Effectively, any activity which focusses pupils' attention on listening to the musical material carefully will help them 'catch' it.

Chunking and teaching by rote

This method of teaching requires you to break down the teaching of a song into smaller chunks for instance by section, e.g. verse/chorus, by phrase, by small units of bars or by individual melodic or rhythmic ideas. You can use this method if you are learning the song by ear and with the notation too.

When you are first teaching a new song to your choir, you will want to think about which section you want to tackle first. You might want to start with the chorus (if it is verse – chorus – verse – chorus form) so that there is something familiar for the group to latch onto that recurs throughout the song. You might want to begin by working with them on internalising the pulse or a particular rhythmic feature – if it is integral to the song, or perhaps particularly tricky. In other words, you won't necessarily want to begin at bar 1 and just plod through it.

A common approach if you're working by ear is to take a verse, for example, then break the verse down into phrases and teach a line at a time. Depending on things like: how long the phrases are, how accustomed your singers are to learn in this way, i.e. how good their ear and musical memory is, and the complexity of the material. You may need to break the phrases down into bite-size pieces that your singers can remember. You might also want to share an audio recording of the song with the singers so they can practise at home and to avoid a lot of note-bashing during rehearsals.

The idea with rote teaching is to sing a line then the singers sing it back to you: 'My turn – your turn' (remembering not to sing with them, but to listen). To make it super clear, it helps if you point to yourself when it's your turn and point to the choir when it's their turn. This approach also allows you to build in the phrasing and expression that you want from the outset. You are setting the singers up to listen to and copy how you sing each phrase and that will extend to more than just the notes and the words. They will mimic your phrasing, note-lengths, vocal style and tone, so you'll be able to achieve far more learning than if you were to play them the phrase on the piano, for example.

Pausing and going over any tricky corners in a bit more detail as you go will help to iron out problems at an early stage. You don't want your choir to learn something with a mistake in it – un-learning a mistake is much harder than learning correctly in the first place. So, take the time to cement the correct learning of each phrase and section as you go. Repetition of the tricky bits with directed listening (e.g. can you hear that the jump in this phrase is bigger than the first phrase? Can you repeat just these few notes after me?) will help with accuracy from the earliest stages of learning. Slowing down complex or fiddly phrases and sections might also help with learning accuracy. You can begin to join the chunks together again once they have been accurately learnt. Over time you can get very good at learning by ear and folk and gospel singers, for instance, have amazing musical memories learning long passages of music very quickly – words and all. Note though that you'll need to recap over sessions if the music is to be memorised.

Using a score

Some choirs learn new repertoire by reading the sheet music. Some very advanced choirs can do this at sight, but it can take a long time to learn this skill even if you already read notation.

Some choirs learn mainly by ear but also have the notation and lyrics to look at. This can be quite a good solution for young singers because using the musical score in combination with rote teaching gives pupils an additional source of reference – the words and the melody written down. You can help your singers to learn to read music by combining rote teaching in combination with reading the notation. This will help pupils to follow the music, see the shape of the melody and make connections with what they are singing and reading. Over time they will gradually begin to recognise elements of notation and be on the road to learning to read it. They will be able to see when the melody rises and falls and relate that to the sound, and will gradually begin to absorb note values, especially with a few pointers from you. It might be that singers can estimate the shape of the melody and rhythm already but not have the level of skill to read as precisely as you'd require, so here, too, you can be helping to improve reading skills whilst ensuring the music is accurately learnt and later read.

Ways into part singing

Rounds

Rounds are the easiest route to part singing. So, if your aim is get your group singing in harmony, then your first job is to teach your pupils how to sing a round.

A round is a song that you can layer up with different groups, each starting at a different designated place. Rounds work because the notes in the melody harmonise at designated moments when the tune is placed over itself. Depending on the song, rounds can work in numerous ways, using two or more parts and starting a beat apart or four beats apart. Rounds usually have a 'star' or some other instruction written above the stave where the different entries come in.

It sounds obvious but a round will only work well if everyone knows the song well. Learn the song over a few sessions and when everyone has memorised the entire song, give it a go. There are different ways to put a round together, here are some ideas:

■ With inexperienced round singers you might first want to try layering up each line. Assign one line to each group and ask them to keep repeating their line once they have entered. Provide a starting pitch and count in; start with line 1, then add line 2, then line 3 etc. This is a good way to experience the parts locking together without singing the song as a full round.

■ First, sing the round through in unison, then break into your round parts. As the parts come in one at a time they should also come to an end one at a time.

■ Alternatively, agree to repeat the round a certain number of times, once the first part has finished, all parts finish. Some will be at the end of line 1, some at line 2 and some will be finishing 3. This takes a bit of practice as it feels odd stopping part way through a song but it can sound very effective once you've mastered conducting the end (and singers know to watch you and stop when it's time).

■ Finally, another interesting way to finish a round and to give a performance a sense of drama, is to create an ostinato based on a short phrase from the song, introducing it the final time through the round. As soon as the first entry finishes their final time through, they begin to sing the ostinato phrase. Once the second entry finishes they join in and so forth, until everyone is singing the ostinato. At this point you can then fade out to silence.

The tricky bit for any leader of a round is to know where you are in the song at any given moment and this takes lots of practice so don't worry if you keep getting lost – it happens all the time. Identify strong and confident singers to be 'part leaders' whose responsibility it is to keep track of how many times through they are and to encourage and support the rest of the singers on the same part.

Partner songs

Partner songs are stand-alone songs that can be sung in combination because their chords/harmony are complementary, so they can be 'mashed up'. Famous songs that fit together are *Swing low, sweet chariot* and *Oh when the saints*, for instance. Partner songs, much like rounds, benefit from everybody learning the song thoroughly before singing them simultaneously. One common thing that can catch you out is the way the songs start. In this case both songs start on an upbeat but each is slightly different. Additionally, the songs start on different notes meaning you'll need to give two groups of singers a different note. Understanding these little details are crucial in teaching and rehearsing the song and are worth practising with singers.

Using your own voice or using a track

If you can hold a tune then model singing yourself – you don't have to have the greatest voice; just lots of enthusiasm. If you really can't sing in tune, use performance and echo style tracks to help you, or by playing the music on a piano, for instance, but make sure they aren't too loud; you need to hear the children sing to give feedback.

> **Tip** ❯ **Not an opera singer? Don't worry.**
>
> Confidence and enthusiasm are key, the children will take their lead from you. You don't need to be an opera singer to lead singing. And you don't need to be able to read music either, nor do you need to be able to play the piano. Sing to the children with a natural, unforced singing voice and with obvious enjoyment and they will be keen to copy you. If you are new to this, set yourself achievable goals of learning and teaching a small number of songs at a time. You will be the role model for the children, so try to sing with an expressive face and with feeling for the words.

Young Singing Leaders

Leadership can be an invaluable experience for children and young people. When young people become leaders, it empowers them to make their own decisions, developing their self-awareness and giving them a range of valuable life skills. It can also allow them to shine in a new environment, making them role models to younger children and respected figures to their peers or adults.

Singing, itself, is a fantastic way of bridging social gaps and improving confidence. It provides an excellent vehicle for young people who want to take on leadership roles. It can make young people feel more self-confident, and improve their social, musical and organisational skills. A joint singing project involving a feeder-primary and a local secondary school can be effective in easing the transition between schools for pupils. It also creates role models, and when younger children see older pupils sing it makes singing aspirational and gives them something to aim for.

A young singing leader is someone between the ages of 5–19 who is leading singing with others. This can be anything from teaching a song in the playground to leading a performance with a choir. Children may actually have experienced leading singing without realising it. If they have taught a song to a classmate or group of friends, they have already had a go at being singing leaders.

The role of the teacher

Young singing leaders should be given ample space to give vocal leadership a try, and feel able to take responsibility, make mistakes, laugh, and reflect on their own progress and that of the rest of the group.

It is also your role to equip the budding young leaders with a good range of techniques. Teach songs and warm-ups using a variety of methods, and encourage the young leaders to reflect on the techniques you are using. Which do they find effective, and which don't work so well? Which would they feel comfortable using to teach someone else a song?

Try to provide a structure with appropriate opportunities for the young leaders to develop their knowledge and skills. Make sure there is a clear distinction between teaching leadership techniques yourself, and stepping back to support the young people to take the lead.

Finally, make sure you are positive and confident when in front of the young leaders. Both qualities are infectious, and we all respond to enthusiastic, passionate and engaging people.

A space to lead

For a young leader to flourish, you need to create a safe, positive, non-judgmental environment in which they are feel able to step outside of their comfort zone and develop their skills. It helps to:

- Set clearly defined boundaries about:
  - The roles and responsibilities of the young leaders
  - The role and responsibilities of adults present
  - The roles, responsibilities and expectations of the singers

- Allow the young leaders to set their own pace of progression
- Give them the opportunity to reflect on the experience of leadership in order to enhance their learning.

Leadership opportunities

Like those learning any new skill, Young Singing Leaders need lots of opportunities to practise and develop. Running dedicated training sessions is a great way of introducing them to new techniques and allowing them to develop their skills.

Other leadership opportunities can be formal or informal, and can take place in a variety of situations:

- The playground at break and lunch time
- Lessons (either in their own class or visiting others)
- Assemblies
- School concerts/shows
- Singing clubs/choir
- With parents and teachers
- Joint sessions with other schools

Considerations when working with Young Singing Leaders

Now you've decided on your own role in training the Young Singing Leaders, and have figured out when and where they will practise, you can take your own approach. This will depend on the particular children you are working with, and on your own aims and aspirations. Use this list of considerations to help inform your decisions:

- What are your aims for working with Young Singing Leaders?
- Who are your young leaders and how are they identified?
- How will you make sure that they have appropriate opportunities to lead?
- How will you know when to stop leading, step back and allow the young leaders to have a go?
- Have you held conversations with the young leaders about how to choose repertoire for other children, considering things like the appropriateness of song lyrics for different age groups, the pitch and the difficulty level?
- Have you held conversations with them about vocal health, e.g. how to teach songs in the playground without shouting and straining your voice?
- How will you consider children's needs and be open-minded to new ideas?
- How will you support personal and group reflection so that young leaders develop their skills and confidence?

Considerations for setting up projects with other schools

Once your Young Singing Leaders are confident in their techniques, visiting other schools to share singing is a great way for them to develop even further, and also to advocate vocal leadership to other young people. Here are some considerations for starting a Young Singing Leaders project with other schools in your area:

- What is the best way to choose and recruit other schools to take part?
- What is the best way to gain support from the senior leadership in your school?
- How is the availability of Young Singing Leaders negotiated to ensure they can attend all sessions?
- Are there issues of transporting pupils to other schools, rehearsals or concert venues?
- What commitment is needed from the school?
- Does the project need a contract or letter of agreement?
- What accredited programmes is the school already involved in? Could these actively support and celebrate young vocal leadership?

Vocal Leader checklist

Bringing it all together

Sing Up's ten principles of good quality vocal leadership underpin the process of becoming a Singing School from the perspective of how the *behaviours* and *actions* of those leading singing affect the quality of the learning and singing. They are based on good principles of teaching and as such will feel like familiar territory for any teacher.

In working with these 10 principles, teachers without a musical specialism are able to develop confidence and expertise in vocal leadership within a progressive and structured framework.

As you read through each principle, think about how you will fulfil each one in your school and write down three ideas. Use the tips to help you.

For more detail on the checklist below go to the product page on fabermusicstore.com.

1 ENGAGING
They are flexible, responsive and share their enthusiasm to create enjoyable, relevant and well-paced sessions.

1.
2.
3.

Tip > Think about the warm-ups and repertoire you pick and the approaches you will use to teach them.

2 SUPPORTIVE
They respect group members, value effort, celebrate achievements and encourage reflection.

1.
2.
3.

Tip > Will every class have the same targets?

3 INCLUSIVE
They enable all group members to participate by taking different abilities into account and respecting everyone's contribution.

1.
2.
3.

Tip > What different methods of communication will you make use of to include everyone?

4 SUPPORTIVE OF PROGRESS

They are willing to try a range of approaches that help people improve, highlighting opportunities for development.

1.

2.

3.

Tip Think about how you can establish a culture of 'how do we improve?' with positive, constructive feedback.

5 EFFECTIVE COMMUNICATORS

They employ appropriate verbal and non-verbal methods of communication, enabling all group members to understand and learn to the best of their abilities.

1.

2.

3.

Tip What effect might your body language and gestures have?

6 CREATIVE

They encourage experimentation and invention, using a range of different approaches and ideas.

1.

2.

3.

Tip Think about how you might include creative voice work – songwriting or group improvisation, for example.

7 COMMITTED TO LEARNING

They are open-minded and eager to learn, taking responsibility for their own continuing professional development.

1.

2.

3.

Tip How do you go about refreshing what you do with new ideas?

8 MUSICAL

They are committed to developing their own musical skills; they embrace a diverse range of music, are able to challenge a group appropriately and find ways to explore different forms of musical expression.

1.

2.

3.

Tip Think about how you could develop your own musical skills in areas such as rehearsal techniques. Who could you go to for advice?

9 COMMUNITY-FOCUSSED

They are committed to an ethos of collaboration, partnership and developing connections.

1.

2.

3.

Tip What opportunities are there to share singing with other schools and groups. Who else can you make connections with?

10 CARING ABOUT THE VOICE

They understand good vocal health and care for the voices of others as well as their own.

1.

2.

3.

Tip Think about what you would advise other teachers or young singers to do to keep their voices healthy.

5

SINGING ACROSS THE SCHOOL DAY, WEEK, YEAR AND BEYOND

When children feel secure and relaxed; when they are unafraid to try new things; when they feel they belong and that they are supported and encouraged by their peers and teachers, they can learn and achieve remarkable things. A culture of singing in your school will help create a positive learning environment that will benefit all those involved.

"We concentrate on pupils' academic achievement but we also concentrate on the pupils' whole development and singing is a very important part of that. Singing makes sure that the two link together: it helps with their confidence, resilience and self-belief, and this is transferred across all areas of their work."

Lynne Thompson, Head Teacher, Trafalgar Infants School

Here is a reminder of some of the benefits of singing:

1. Singing oxygenates the blood, aiding brain function, and engages many areas of the brain simultaneously.
2. It creates a focussed activity that the students all take part in together.
3. Information in the form of lyrics helps with memorisation – it's easy to learn things when you sing them.
4. Singing is an ideal stress-buster, releasing endorphins and aiding our immune system. This can be a real help around pressurised exam periods.
5. It is enjoyable and will make the students feel good. Nothing unites a group of individuals like singing together.

Embedding singing across the school day

So how do you start? The answer is with small steps that everyone can manage easily. A commitment to singing in school doesn't need to be an additional activity that you need to make time for.

Routine songs

Think about what you already do, every day, in your classroom and elsewhere in the school. Now think about instead of using your speaking voice, switching it out to a singing voice. You are already doing these things, so it takes no extra time to do them through singing. Think of it a bit like switch diet for a healthier lifestyle – fruit instead of chocolate – except in this exchange you are swapping something routine, maybe monotonous and every-day for something much more engaging and enjoyable!

Embedding singing through routine songs is a really good place to start that won't disrupt your day or your lesson-planning. You can punctuate the school day with bursts of singing that will help with transition moments from one activity to another with your class. For example:

- A 'Hello' song in the morning
- Lining up
- Singing the register
- Circle time
- Tidying up
- Time to wash our hands
- Star of the day
- A 'Goodbye' song at the end of the school day

Hello song

Singing a simple 'Hello' song with the children every morning is a great way to make sure that everyone feels welcome and part of the community. If someone sings your name to you, it makes you feel like you belong. If you have new pupils at the school, pupils who are struggling to settle in and make friends, or perhaps you have children whose family circumstances mean they move schools frequently, having some things that happen as a routine in the school every day can help these new pupils to be assimilated and become part of the fabric of the school quite quickly.

For children who don't have English as their first language coming into the school, by incorporating some daily singing routines they can learn the tune and understand the meaning of something simple like a 'Hello' song. Singing this regularly will help them begin to acquire the language.

Lining up

Using a song helps to establish routines, like lining up more quickly and easily, especially with younger children. Singing is enjoyable and keeps children 'busy' so helps with behaviour management too.

Sing the register

One of the best kept routines in school is calling the register – it's the perfect place to start embedding a little singing in the day.

- Begin by singing: "Let's sing the register" to G, EA, GG, E or 'so, me-la, so-so, me' (the playground taunt: 'na na nee na-na na').
- Then sing each child's name to G, E or 'so, me,' e.g. "Al-ex".
- Each child responds with "here –", or "here I am" to the same notes.

You can expand the range of notes you use for this over time as you and the children become more confident. It is a call-and-response format anyway, so they will naturally mimic what you do in the 'call' with each of their names.

Circle time

Creating new lyrics to a well-known tune, like a nursery rhyme, provides a brand-new song and supports daily routines, such as making a circle. Try the tune of *Frère Jacques* with these lyrics as a starting point: "Make a circle, make a circle, everyone, everyone, sit down on the carpet, sit down on the carpet, great, well done, great, well done."

> "I noticed that it's this sort of moment when you might lose the children's attention and have to reinforce good behaviour. I discovered that simply by singing together you had every child on board in a positive, enjoyable way."
>
> Rachel O'Hara, Teacher, Chase Bridge Primary School

Tidying up

A singing voice cuts above the general sound of the classroom and can be heard easily as a cue for pupils to join in. The tidying up song in the Song Bank breaks down the whole task into separate parts, i.e. "books are closed, pencils put away, rulers collected, it's a busy day". Using a song, which has a time frame keeps pupils on task and challenges them to finish quickly and effectively.

Time to wash our hands

After a while, songs become internalised and this can help reinforce positive behaviours. By memorising the lyrics and tune of a washing-our-hands song (composed by you and your class) it will remind pupils of the necessary steps each time they come to wash their hands. The repetitive nature also helps support SEND and EAL (English as an additional language) pupils. The Sing Up *Washing hands* song is to the tune of *Skip to my lou*. Try creating your own version.

Star of the day song

With Early Years and Key Stage 1 children, you could initiate a 'Star of the day' scheme to recognise and reward good behaviours and habits. Sing to the tune of *Skip to my lou*.

"Star, star, star of the day, star, star, star of the day
Star, star, star of the day, today is Charlie Davis."

You could create a poster for the child to take home telling them why they were the star of the day.

You can involve the other children in your decision: "Who do you think has been the star of the day?" If the teacher has been commenting during the day about the good things that child has been doing, praising the child, the other children will have picked up on that.

Goodbye song

Having a memorable and uplifting end to a lesson or the school day will help children (and staff) leave on a positive note! It helps create a moment of calm reflection, where we acknowledge the people we've spent the day with, what's been achieved and thank our school staff and friends. It reinforces the use of greetings and manners and like any singing, helps to build a cohesive school community.

Singing for changing the dynamic in the room

There are times in the school day when you will want to wake your class up and make them more alert and energetic, and there are other times when you will need them to be calm and focussed. Your choice of song at these points can help you achieve this.

You might want to try an energising physical and vocal warm-up to get

---

Song Bank suggestions

Come and sit down

Hello, how are you?

The lining up song

It's time to have our break

Woah! I need your attention!

We're feeling very whingy

The tidying up song

Have you got your book bag?

The goodbye song

It's time to go

---

everyone bright and alert. Singing a calming, relaxing song together can calm everyone down after playtime and get them into the right frame of mind for some reading or quiet work.

Singing together lowers our heart-beat which is also good for calming down, relaxing and de-stressing. Repetition of daily routines can also be quite comforting for children, particularly for those with some types of special needs. Singing something familiar and repetitive but making small changes to it, like volume, speed, etc., can be useful for focussing attention on detail.

Older pupils

Any simple, short tasks that are part of your daily classroom routine can be turned into a singing moment. This works best if you get pupils into the habit from the outset, and some of these songs will feel more appropriate to Early Years and Key Stage 1 children (4–7 year olds) than they will with your older children. But starting here will mean that by the time they move to Key Stage 2 (7–11 year olds), they will be in the singing habit, and singing can be embedded in their school day in other ways at that point.

As pupils move into KS2, the singing you do has to grow with them. This will be where the role of Young Singing Leaders comes to the fore and they can begin to lead the singing themselves. The children will be developing the skills to write their own simple songs – take a well-known tune and ask them to write alternative lyrics for a routine or task that they choose, for example.

From age seven, they begin to have more to remember at home time – their book bag, their water bottle, PE kit – and this is the age at which their parent or carer who is collecting them probably won't be helping them with this. So, a simple 'home time' song incorporating these reminders will be helpful.

With older pupils the style of the songs you choose will also change. You can develop raps or chants and link English work to song-writing – if the pupil is writing the song they will have to make sure it rhymes and the words fit the melody.

Singing to aid learning

As academic pressure and curriculum content ramps up in KS2, so can pupil stress and fatigue. Using little vocal warm-ups for a brain-break can be really helpful. A simple sing-along for a few minutes can really brighten the room and make everyone smile while releasing tension and stress. Also, it is in this learning stage where you can really maximise the benefits to learning through singing. Think about songs as 'diving in' points, to help you enrich and learn about a topic and bring it to life. The rhyme, rhythm and repetition of songs help you remember the lyrics which can contain useful facts and aid memory. If you prepare for a topic assembly with your pupils, include songs based around that topic. Your pupils will have thought about it, learned it, researched it, put it together and performed it for someone else – making for a deep learning process.

Singing assemblies

School assemblies are traditionally a time for collective worship. They are a focal point for the whole school community and are an important opportunity to explore themes and values such us friendship, resilience, kindness, responsibility, respect, tolerance etc. They also provide a moment of calm, a time to celebrate, a space for reflection and an opportunity to sing together.

Collective singing within this context gives an additional binding layer of expression and meaning to the exploration of faith and values. It can also be a way of touching on and opening discussion around difficult subjects like bereavement, conflict resolution, coming to terms with change, or difficulties at home. Of course, there will also be celebration assemblies for particular events and times of year, like Harvest, Christmas, Easter etc., all of which will include singing.

Reaping the benefits of collective singing

Pupils and staff sharing and enjoying singing together regularly has a very positive impact on cohesion within the school community. Songs become the soundtrack of your childhood and are embedded in the memory for a surprisingly long time – often for life. Many young people leave messages on Sing Up's website saying how much they loved singing particular songs at primary school, and they remember who taught the song to them or who they used to sing it with. As the late neurologist and author Oliver Sacks said in his book *Musicophilia*, humans have an "extraordinary tenacity of musical memory, so that much of what is heard during one's early years may be 'engraved' on the brain for the rest of one's life".[11]

During a school assembly, children from different classes and year-groups are brought together in a common experience and share an activity with purpose and endeavour. It is a contrasting moment in a school day and an opportunity for teachers to engage with the children in a different way from the classroom environment.

How can you get the most from your singing assemblies?

Let's start by turning this question on its head. What is your assembly for and how can you incorporate singing to maximise the value and deepen the experience for your pupils?

- It might be an opportunity to allow pupils to experience music they might not otherwise hear. Music from different times and places will broaden their internal musical 'library' and widen their musical horizons.
- You might incorporate a vocal warm-up to get everyone relaxed and ready for singing.
- You could have some 'school songs', i.e. ones that are familiar to the school and carry some meaning about the school's ethos and values.

> "They're so happy, and you feel like this is the one time you've got 330 children and they're all with you and they're all singing their hearts out and it's quite a unique thing."
>
> Rachel O'Hara, Teacher, Chase Bridge Primary School

■ The act of singing together can instil some of the qualities you want to support children to develop, for example, respect, kindness and consideration. This is, in part, because singing is an act of very personal self-expression as well as a communal activity.

■ You might want to incorporate a moment of weekly celebration where certificates are given out and achievements are celebrated, and have a song to sing to enable everyone present to sing their congratulations.

■ For a topic assembly, there is no better springboard than a well-chosen song. It will help not only to cement the knowledge but also create an engaging performance for the audience, whether they are pupils or parents.

CASE STUDY

The whole school learns a new song weekly in Singing Assembly. Every year group has class singing lessons and class teachers use songs in their lessons to introduce new topics. Nearly 200 children participate in weekly choir practices and 40 children have group singing lessons. There are also 25 Young Singing Leaders who lead playground singing. The children have opportunities throughout the year to perform to different sized audiences in a variety of venues.

Catherine Andrews, Highfield Junior School, Bromley

Singing-practice assemblies

Assemblies which are specifically set aside for collective singing practice are fantastic for learning and rehearsing new songs for future assemblies, shows, nativities, leavers' assemblies, concerts and other special events. They are also opportunities to improve and refine the quality of the singing and how well the songs are known. Try the following:

■ Split singing-practice assemblies into age-groups so you can focus on songs at an appropriate level of difficulty to match the children's ability.

■ Work with your Young Singing Leaders to help lead some of the singing.

■ Get into the habit of reflecting on the quality of the sound and give pupils the opportunity to listen for good singing themselves and to be aware of how they sound (refer to Chapter 9: *Making progress and improving singing* for suggestions).

■ Get colleagues to help. You don't want to be focussed on crowd control, you want to focus on the singing.

In an ideal world, the best-case scenario for singing-practice assemblies would be for you to have a big open space, where no-one is coming and going, which is light and airy (not too hot or cold) and which has space to sit and stand comfortably.

Other considerations

Accompaniment

Will you use live or recorded accompaniment? Ideally, you would use both and include some *a cappella* singing as well. Is there a piano and someone to play it? Is there good quality audio equipment?

Leading

Who is leading? Are there adults (parents, other staff) and Young Singing Leaders who can help? For example, you can be leading the singing from the front while someone else plays the piano or takes care of the audio equipment for you. If you are leading inclusive singing in a Special School or with SEND pupils, you will need additional adults who might sign, lead actions or focus on particular pupils to ensure they are included and engaged.

Repertoire

What repertoire will you choose? A whole-school assembly needs songs that are accessible to a wide age range, potentially from EYFS to KS2, and they would ideally appeal to teachers too. You will want to develop a collection of songs that reflects your school community, that are catchy, not too wordy and in a range of styles and moods. Songs that celebrate your school values and uplift your community will make for joyous singing occasions.

Goals

Establish some objectives early on and think about what you want to achieve over, for example, a six-week period. Try and get a balance between being thorough but also keeping up the pace.

Challenge and development

An effective singing practice will consist of:

- A physical and vocal warm-up to get everybody ready for singing
- Repetition of something familiar – perhaps the rehearsal of a chorus that was learnt the previous week
- Something new – building on the familiar, such as learning the verse to go with the chorus they already know
- A challenge – such as adding dynamics to the piece, learning a harmony line, trying to sign the chorus in sign language or Makaton, working on articulation of the lyrics, focusing on facial expression to tell the story and convey emotions etc.
- A mini performance – putting together the separate components and creating a mini performance which brings together the work of the previous weeks
- Feedback – pinpoint and shine a light on good vocal health techniques, quality singing and expressive singing.

Singing and religion

There are strong connections and traditions of choirs singing as part of collective worship. Indeed, the Christian church in the Middle Ages tried to suppress singing for anything other than religious purposes. But from the Middle Ages onwards, secular songs have also been popular. Troubadours, or travelling musicians, had been spreading music among the population on their travels since the 11th century. They avoided spiritual or religious themes focussing instead on love, joy and pain – frequently rooted in a form of popular story-telling.

When your school comes together for a moment of collective worship, whether you are in a faith school, or a secular school, what you might choose to sing in those moments will vary depending on the backgrounds and beliefs of your pupils. You may have children from a variety of faiths so some sensitivity to those differences is going to be something to think about when you choose songs to sing together. Rather than avoiding singing any songs that are from particular religions, you might choose to include songs from all the religions which are represented within your pupil cohort. This can be a really nice way to integrate pupils within the wider community and to spread understanding and awareness of different cultures and beliefs within the school. In other words, you can sing Christmas carols at Christmas, and also sing Jewish songs at Hanukkah, and Hindu songs to celebrate Diwali. Parents and grandparents of children at the school from these faiths will be a great source of traditional songs, and can be invited into the school to teach them to the children and explain the meaning and stories behind them.

Singing and Islam[12]

There is often a misconception that all singing is 'haram' or prohibited in Islam. Most scholars of Islam agree that this is untrue, but there are varying interpretations of the rules from different Islamic communities. There are certain kinds of singing and contexts for singing which are prohibited and some which are not, so you should be able to include your Muslim pupils in at least some of the singing you do at school. If you have Muslim children within your school for whom taking part in singing seems to be an issue, do talk to your local Imam to find out more detail about what is appropriate if you are unsure.

Prohibited 'Haram' singing:

- Singing which contains a celebration of the material world or which includes sexual connotation.
- Singing which includes text that would be inappropriate for speaking – swearing, sexually explicit language etc.
- Singing which removes the person away from worship and appropriate presence with Allah or towards ignoring one's rights and responsibilities.
- Singing habitually or purely for fun can be problematic for some Muslims.

Permitted 'Halal' singing:

- Singing which glorifies Allah.
- Singing about goodness or happiness – singing that soothes the heart in a Halal manner, e.g. for festivals and weddings. You will likely find that most of the songs you want to sing in primary school that relate to peace, kindness, friendship and other positive values, are permitted.
- Singing which is general – not prohibited nor specifically about goodness and happiness – is permitted within its context. As long as it doesn't lead an individual to ignore their rights and responsibilities.
- Singing for a purpose – classroom singing to support learning may fit within this context.

Additionally, in some instances, unaccompanied singing is permitted whilst singing accompanied by instruments is not. There is a hadith (a saying of the Prophet) which forbids the playing of stringed and wind instruments. Sometimes this is taken to include any pitched instrument. The context for this hadith relates to the use of instruments in licentious settings, indeed the Arabic word for 'music' relates to entertainment of low moral quality and self-indulgence and for some Muslims the only acceptable instruments are the voice and unpitched percussion. Most Muslim children before puberty are allowed to play instruments and sing but as they move into adolescence the playing of pitched instruments in particular can become more problematic for stricter Muslims.

Where are the opportunities to sing across the school day?

You don't want a completely structured day – your pupils need some downtime too, but there are also opportunities to slot little bits of singing in to punctuate the school day as you go. You don't need to be doing all of these. They are just examples to give you some ideas.

▷ Breakfast clubs

1. Arriving in the classroom
2. A 'Hello' song
3. Singing the register
4. Physical warm-up
5. Time to sit down

▷ Morning lessons

1. Mental starters – brain gym singing activities
2. Maths – singing your times tables, maths songs
3. English – specific songs, grammar songs, songs for World Book Day.

▷ Next lesson

1. A song to calm and focus after playtime ready for learning
2. A tidy up song at the end before lunch

▷ Break-time

1. Lining up song
2. Playground singing games
3. A singing stop in the playground for spontaneous singing
4. Young Singing Leaders leading playground singing games

Lunchtime

1. Singing clubs
2. Choir practice
3. Young Singing Leaders learning new songs ready to teach them to others

Afternoon lessons

1. An energising song to counteract the post-lunch slump
2. Topic-based songs as ways into learning
3. Circle time – forming a circle, and songs for singing in circle time, perhaps to go with a story

End of the school day

1. Star of the day song
2. Tidying up song
3. 'Have you got your book bag?' reminder song
4. 'Goodbye' song
5. End of day sing-along

After school

1. Singing staff meetings – have a sing-along!
2. Share and teach new songs to the whole staff after school – have a 'song of the week' that you teach to staff on a Monday after school
3. Practise some songs for the staff to sing to the children in assembly
4. Form a staff choir – invite parents and governors
5. Hold a piece of singing training led by your music teacher or by a visiting specialist

Playground singing[13]

Children have been using outdoor singing to get moving and have fun for centuries, and it's likely that there is already a lot of it happening in your school playground – have a listen out to see what you can hear. With our tips you can make even more of the singing in your school playground.

Explore playground traditions

Task the children with asking parents and grandparents what songs they remember from their own playground days, which can then be shared at school. You'll be able to see commonalities with popular playground songs now. Clapping games have always been popular, and many songs have historical or political themes that can be explored to find out about the past.

Let your singing leaders lead the way

There are many ways of selecting and empowering Young Singing Leaders at school, but one thing you can be sure of is that there will be plenty of volunteers. You can buddy older children with younger children and make a rota so everyone knows whose day of the week it is to get singing going in the playground.

Set your stage

Use a Singing Stop or designated singing area, so that everyone knows this is where singing happens. You may be surprised how popular that part of the playground becomes. If you can make that area a sound garden or stage, fantastic, but just a simple marker works well too.

Learn the songs in the classroom first

With general playground noise to contend with, you might want to protect your voice by learning the songs in the quiet of the classroom before taking them outside. Once some children have picked them up, they'll spread like wildfire.

Once you've learnt a song, change it

Like anything learnt through the aural tradition, playground songs often change depending on who you learnt them from and what part of the country you live in. Changing the words to songs is a great way to nurture creativity, and like with any song writing, helps children to develop music and literacy skills.

Get your whole school involved

Teachers, those on lunch duty, teaching assistants, parents and governors can all take part in playground songs and games.

Tip	Good foundations

Whatever the context in which you are singing, it is still important to sing well. Everything we have covered in other chapters about posture, breathing, vocal health and musicianship are equally important in the classroom, in assembly or in the staffroom as they are when you are rehearsing the choir.

School timetable

Next, think about your school and map out what singing across the school day you would like to get going.

Put them into this timetable below:

Time	Monday	Tuesday

Wednesday	Thursday	Friday

Singing across the school year

What are the moments that mark a school year which singing can augment? When are the moments you have the largest number of people in the building? These are your community moments and an opportunity for the children to welcome the wider community into their school.

Welcoming new pupils to the school

- Teaching them the school's songs
- Having a 'welcome' assembly with singing
- Older pupils teaching songs to new pupils
- Songs to help teachers get to know new pupils and establish effective 'new term' routines

Harvest

- A Harvest assembly or concert
- Parents invited in
- Singing in the local community
- Singing about themes connected with Harvest – sharing, generosity, gratitude, the environment

Halloween

- Spooky singing assembly
- Dressing up

Hanukkah, Diwali and Christmas

- Nativities
- Concerts
- Assemblies
- Singing outside school in the local community

Springtime and Easter

- Songs about new beginnings and rebirth
- Songs about nature and the planet

End-of-year concerts, assemblies and events

- Leavers' concerts and prize-givings
- Transition singing projects between primary and secondary schools – shared concerts
- School shows or productions
- Celebrations of the year's work, sharing the songs we have learnt together

Next, think about your school year and map out what singing highpoints across the school year you would like to see happening or which already happen.

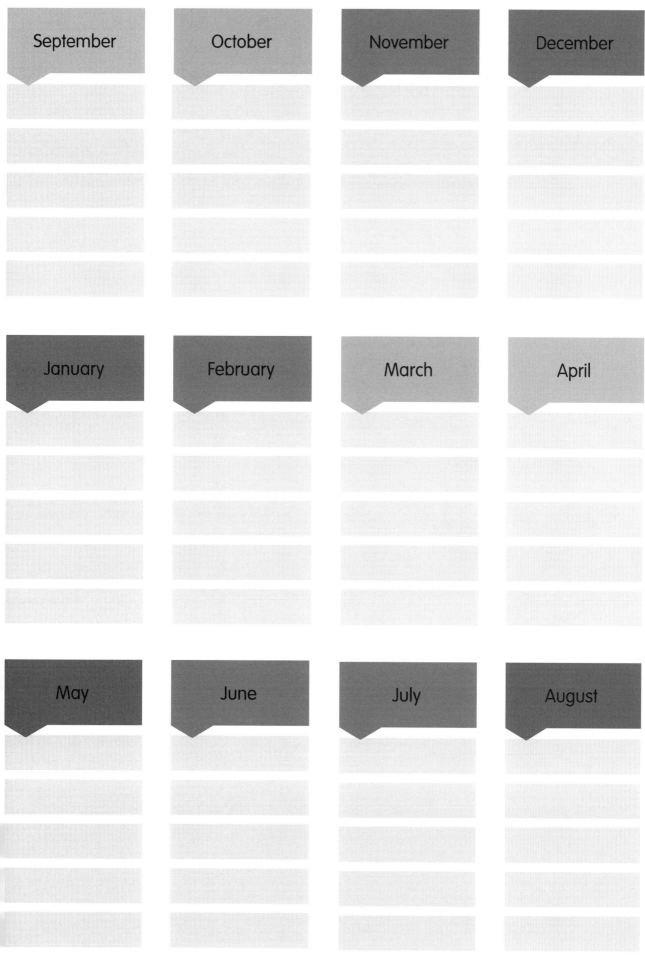

September

October

November

December

January

February

March

April

May

June

July

August

71

Singing around the school

Imagine walking around your school and visualise what singing activity you would like to see and hear in the following places and situations.

On the school bus

In lesson time

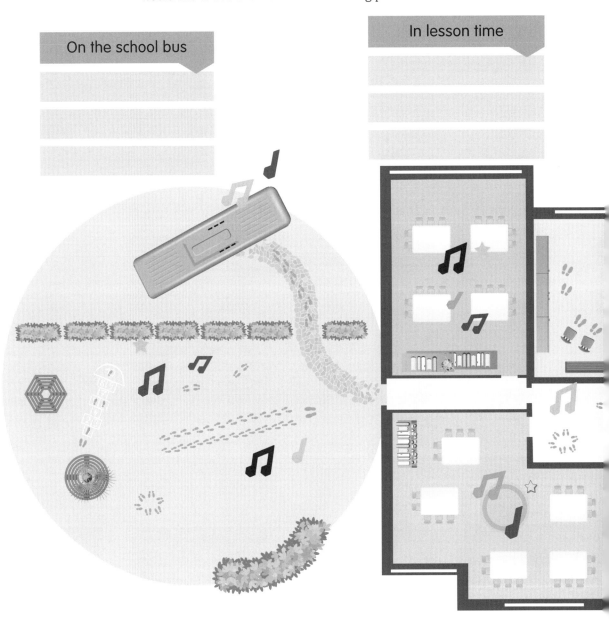

In the playground

Over breakfast club

During morning registration

In assembly

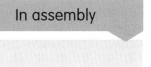

During lunchtime

In the staff room

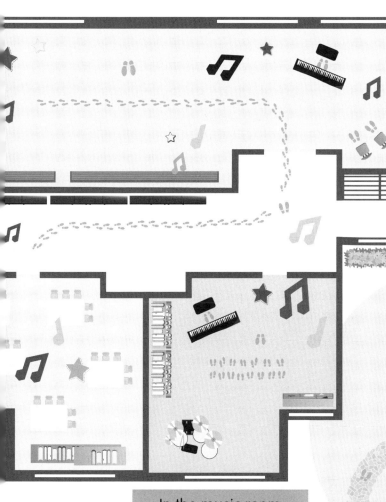

In the music room

After school

6

INCLUSIVE SINGING FOR SPECIAL EDUCATIONAL NEEDS AND DISABILITIES[14]

Singing is for everyone, and an important part of our role as teachers and singing leaders is to take steps to remove barriers to music making and singing for all children, including those who are 'labelled' as having a special educational need.

As educators, we need to ensure we are delivering good practice for *everyone*. Music has the power to break down barriers, but it can also present barriers for some children if we are not careful. With singing, this needs particularly close attention, as the use of words, and of the voice at all, can be inaccessible to some children. Reading and notation can also present challenges, as can the social setting of group singing and the perceived vulnerability of our own individual singing voices. However, there are ways around all of these potential obstacles, and singing can be a hugely inspiring, motivating and positive experience for all.

SEND is a catch-all term covering a very wide range of needs. Within this you will come across a range of labels: learning difficulties, PMLD (Profound and Multiple Learning Difficulties), MLD (Moderate Learning Difficulty), SLD (Severe Learning Difficulties), ASD (Autism Spectrum Disorder), SpLD (Specific Learning Difficulties e.g. dyslexia), additional needs, physically disabled, learning disabled and many more. More social contexts are using alternative language to avoid people becoming identified solely by labels and advocating for the social model of disability – the concept that people are disabled by barriers in society that restrict their life choices.

> "It's an all-inclusive attitude to singing that is key. Everyone can sing, and the whole purpose of singing is everyone coming together and expressing themselves."
>
> Brian Ostro, Deputy Head Teacher, Chase Bridge Primary School

The SEND code of practice defines four main areas of need:

- Communication and interaction
- Social and emotional
- Cognition and learning
- Sensory

In reality, these areas are likely to overlap, and children may be affected to different degrees across different areas of learning. Schools may specialise in terms of need, e.g. visual impairment, autism and communication difficulties, social, emotional and behavioural difficulties, although often children may have a range of needs. Learning disability and physical disability are often connected too, especially within PMLD.

Every child is so unique in their ways to engage and respond that no categorisation can completely and adequately inform your approach.

You will find the best ways to connect with individuals simply through getting to know them. Further to this, as a music leader in particular, it is not always necessary – or possible in the case of some peripatetic teachers visiting for the first time – to be completely aware of each child's label, only how to offer a safe musical space that they can participate in. It may be more useful for a music leader to look at the potential challenges that can be common across many of these categories. One of the most significant things for the music leader to consider will be whether the group or individuals are verbal, nonverbal or preverbal – noting that if they are "nonverbal" it doesn't necessarily mean they do not vocalise, and therefore can't sing.

It is also worth considering how music is built into the day and how this fits into the school setting. There is always a dialogue to be had around the pros and cons of 'inclusive' and 'exclusive' groupings – whether it is better to integrate disabled children into groups of non-disabled children, or to provide small and closely supported sessions specifically targeted at certain learning needs. The teacher is best placed to consider what will work in their setting and for the needs of the children they are working with.

In this chapter, we will explore some of the main barriers for children with special educational needs, and how we can overcome these and provide inclusive singing spaces.

> ### CASE STUDY
>
> The children at the Highfield Schools are incredibly proud of their singing. Children embrace singing because it is completely inclusive. A child doesn't have to be academically gifted to sing well. I can work with 30 children for a year and have absolutely no idea of their academic ability. In fact, some of the best singers and performers that I have worked with are often those who struggle with reading and writing but have an amazing ear and can pick up tunes, rhythms and lyrics with great speed and sensitivity. For these children singing is crucial for their confidence and sense of identity.
>
> Catherine Andrews, Choir Leader, Highfield Schools

Singing for children with cognitive, learning, communication and interaction difficulties

Although we can consider cognitive and learning difficulties as a separate category to communication and interaction difficulties, it can be helpful to the music teacher to approach them in a connected way, as these types of learning difficulty tend to overlap and are not necessarily clearly defined in a child's experience.

Challenges for students

Within these categories you will find Autism, Asperger Syndrome, Dyslexia, Dyspraxia, Global Developmental Delay and a huge variety of specific and non-specific learning difficulties. These could affect a young person's experience in a huge variety of ways that could cause challenges in a music setting.

Use of language

Language can be a huge barrier for children across all areas of education and daily life. This could include their ability to understand spoken and written language, as well as their ability to articulate their thoughts and feelings into speech. They may face challenges in physically producing sounds, or remembering information expressed through language. Some may also *choose* not to speak or use verbal language. For children on the autism spectrum in particular, the use of conceptual, metaphorical or idiomatic language can be confusing as it does not have a direct or literal meaning.

Reading and processing symbols

Reading can be a particularly challenging area, and this can extend to the whole concept of processing visual symbols into information. Notation can be a huge barrier in this way, and any other system where symbols have a meaning that needs to be learnt and understood.

Processing speed

Children may process information more slowly and require more time to respond. This could be auditory, visual or even sensory information, and could relate to instructions, communication, learning tasks or general in-the-moment experiences.

Memory

Many learning difficulties have associated problems with memory. This could affect how a child can retain information long-term or short-term, and consequently affect their ability to learn. It is also extremely common for working memory to be affected, so processing information, instructions, conversation, or a lot of words in the moment could be a significant challenge.

Focus

An extremely common challenge which can be found across almost all learning difficulties is the ability to focus and concentrate for sustained periods, or in certain ways, or on certain things.

Organisation and sequencing

Particularly linked to dyslexia and the autism spectrum, the concept of understanding complex sequences of actions can present challenges, to varying degrees. This could relate to things such as understanding directions and finding your way, understanding how to complete a learning activity, or it could affect routine actions such as getting dressed or putting shoes on.

Social challenges

This is primarily associated with Asperger's and the autism spectrum but could affect any child. Children may struggle to function in a group and to interact with others. Children on the autism spectrum may find it difficult to interpret the communication of others, especially nonverbal aspects, such as body language, facial expression and tone of voice. Those with social, emotional and mental health issues might also struggle with social interaction, often either not being able to control their responses and emotions or withdrawing and being unable to interact.

Sensory sensitivity

Again, usually associated with the autism spectrum, children may have sensitivities to certain sensory triggers. These could be sudden loud noises, bright lights, smells or touch. Environments can provide sensory overload if there is too much information, such as places where there are a lot of things to look at, or lots of noise.

Motor control

Many children may have affected fine or gross motor control, which may affect their ability to sing, clap, use their bodies, produce or respond to rhythm or play musical instruments.

Challenges for classroom teachers

The main challenge for classroom teachers is how to find a way to effectively engage everyone in the room. Children will be learning and processing information at different speeds and responding in different ways. It can be tempting to pitch to the middle and leave some behind, and others 'bored'.

In addition, education resources can rely heavily on language, which can be immediately divisive. Finding resources that are truly inclusive for all learning styles and needs can be a big challenge. There will always be a challenge of holding the group dynamic and balancing the highly different needs of individuals within this, making sure everyone feels safe and valued. If one or two children are not engaged or have a reluctance to sing, then this can affect the whole group. If there are children in the class who are sensitive to sound, this can seemingly present a difficult issue in a music or singing session. It is often the case that these children simply get excluded from the session. It is worth mentioning here, however, that sound sensitivity is rarely a problem in a well set-up music session. The kinds of sounds that tend to have a negative affect are those that are sudden, loud and abrasive, at an unprecedented and unprepared for level of volume, that represent some sort of sound chaos, or something disturbing and repetitive. There can also be specific sounds that are individual to learners – all of these are easily avoided in a session once you are aware of them.

Singing activities

Singing can be a successful and rich approach to working with children with a wide range of learning difficulties. The most important part of the teacher's approach is to view singing as a wide and flexible activity. Singing can provide an inclusive space for children to engage with in their own ways, on many more levels than simply learning and reproducing a song.

Some students may be able to vocalise melody but not words. Sometimes vocalising can be the only opportunity certain learners have to communicate, particularly those with more profound needs. This can be a life-changing experience for them as it may be the only time they have control over what is happening and they are able to communicate and interact in a way that is meaningful to them. Some may enjoy joining in with key words, not necessarily melody. Some will enjoy the ritual of a song, the stops and starts, and the anticipation. Some will join in physically with actions and/or signing. Some may vocalise nonverbal sounds, perhaps with a recognition of pitch. Some may engage in listening and responding physically. Some children could take on other roles within the session, such as choosing songs, conducting, or being in charge of the controls on the CD player.

It is also important to accept and embrace a slower process of engagement. Some students may simply take longer than others to become involved in music and singing, for example it is not fair to assume that if a young person is not immediately joining in that they are not engaged or absorbing what is happening.

Singing and movement games

Singing games are an invaluable resource in most settings. They should offer a range of ways to engage within one game. One activity that can be used in special needs schools as well as many early years settings is called *Playing in a circle*. It simply involves singing the words "playing in a circle" on a melody of two notes, four times in a row, then saying "stop" with a big Makaton stop signal (See 'Makaton', page 87). At the same time the group can be playing instruments all together. This game is incredibly simple but allows for multiple variations. We can play and sing quietly, loudly, fast or slowly. Children can play or sing or dance or be in charge of the stop signal. This could be equally effective with a group of nonverbal children responding to the staff in the room singing. There is value in singing yourself rather than using recordings. It is easier for the children to match a voice than an instrument, and even more so with people and voices that are already familiar to them.

You can also use a movement song on a CD or backing track. This is something to consider where there is a very mixed group of verbal and nonverbal children. Often the emphasis here will be on the game and the movements and you don't necessarily need to teach the song, but simply sing along to it yourself. Over a number of weeks, some children may join in with the singing and others will be engaged in the game and movements, allowing for children to participate to their own level.

Songwriting

You can try some simple song-writing activities with classes, as it can build up a lot of pride and ownership which can lead to a deeper level of engagement. You might bring the beginning of a song with a chorus or theme, e.g. the summer. From there, the input from the group will depend on time, language abilities and age etc.

As an example, with a group of 10 to 11-year-old verbal children, you could ask them all to make up their own short fragments of phrases or melodies, or both. They can then demonstrate their fragments, while you record it and you can then structure this into a song, perhaps for performing to the rest of their school at the end of term. On a much simpler level, with a younger group of mainly nonverbal children, you could ask them to draw pictures of their favourite activities which you can then put into a song that adults could sing and they could play instruments along to. It is also fine to use existing melodies that you and the children know as starting points for creativity and new ideas.

Teaching a song

There is no reason why teaching a set song should be avoided in these settings, and this can be very effective, when prepared in a way that is appropriate and accessible for the group. It is usually a good idea to use a combination of learning aids to support a variety of learning styles, and to build up very slowly whilst still keeping it fun. For example, you may teach the song aurally, by asking the group to copy first the words and then the words with the melody. However, care needs to be taken, as concentrating on the words might put some learners off if they particularly struggle with language. This depends on the group you are working with of course.

Creating bespoke songs

It can often be hard to find the perfect song for a group or for an occasion and many teachers spend hours searching the internet or leafing through songbooks. It can be a good idea in this case to write your own. Think of vocabulary that the children will be familiar with, keep the melody very simple and repetitive, and incorporate ideas or images that the children can directly relate to, e.g. the name of their class, where they live, activities that take place in school. Students can also be involved in the process of writing or inspiring the melody and rhythm of the song, providing individual sounds, phrases or actions during sessions. These can be repeated and incorporated into the song by the teacher, or used in samples if you have an iPad and appropriate apps, or a loop pedal, for example.

Using singing to teach other musical elements

Songs can also be used to teach other musical elements. When teaching the ukulele to a class of children on the autism spectrum, you could create a song naming all the different parts of the instrument, or a song that names the chords or strings as you strum them. You could also try using songs that give words to different drum rhythms, which classes can play at the same time as sing. Another variation is a turn-taking song, where the whole group sings a chorus, then leaves a space for one child to take a free instrumental solo. The lyrics can help to encourage listening, respecting and celebrating the person taking their turn.

Singing for transitions

Singing can be extremely helpful for transitions, which can be challenging moments during the school day for many children with learning difficulties, particularly those on the autism spectrum. In a music session with these children, you might want to begin with a welcome song, or a song introducing the fact that it is now "music time", and end with a "goodbye" or a "music is finished" song.

Technology

Many special needs schools use BIGmac switches for nonverbal children, onto which they can record fragments of speech such as a name or "good morning" that they can use to contribute to communication or singing activities. Microphones can be used to enhance vocal sounds. Not all learners like this, but many respond much better when their voices are amplified or effects are applied to them. If the speaker is close to them, this is also another way of reinforcing a sense of self. Using an effect on the voice can be particularly effective for autistic learners and those with low self-esteem or who are shy, as it is not *exactly* their own voice that can be heard. This can be a great way to get reluctant students vocalising.

IMPROVED UNDERSTANDING OF MUSIC

J is a nine-year-old with learning difficulties and very limited verbal communication. In early music lessons he showed considerable enjoyment and his level of musical participation involved starting and stopping playing at roughly the right time. Over several months we worked on drumming and singing simple patterns and songs. Gradually J began to sing certain words at the right point in the songs and play the rhythm of the word on the drum at the same time. He was then able to take these fragments of rhythm and play them on the drum as a contribution during other activities. His sense of pulse, rhythm and pitch developed hugely.

DEVELOPING INTERACTION SKILLS AND FACILITATING PARTICIPATION

O is on the autism spectrum and at first was overwhelmed by joining in a new group singing setting, crying and asking to leave the room. The session began with a welcome song that used the names of everyone in the room. When O heard his name in the song he responded with a smile. Each session he became more confident during this singing moment, coming to anticipate his name being sung, and being ready with a smile and a wave for the rest of the group.

INCREASING CREATIVITY AND EXPLORATION

P is four years old with cognitive and learning difficulties. At first he was disengaged during songs which encouraged each child to take turns to have a solo moment. He would pick up a drum and make a few small sounds. However, with repetition, and the space and silence to hear and appreciate his own explorations, he began to use his voice. He started to explore sounds, syllables and pitches, creating his own songs and then adding drum rhythms to them at the same time.

PROVIDING OPPORTUNITIES TO SHOW POTENTIAL THAT MAY NOT BE RECOGNISED IN OTHER SUBJECT AREAS

A (nine years old) had learning difficulties and extremely limited verbal communication and could often seem disengaged in activities. Due to slow processing speeds he was often unable to contribute to group activities in the classroom. However in music and singing activities that were repeated consistently over a period of time, A would begin to join in with some of the words of songs, showing that he was in fact processing and learning the music. This developed into him spontaneously contributing sung musical ideas within creative processes that were sustained and repeated over time.

Tip ⟩⟩ **Top Tips on cognitive, learning, communication and interaction difficulties**

1. Link as many concepts and learning styles together as possible within one activity e.g. visual, auditory, kinaesthetic, linguistic.

2. Use technology like microphones, loop pedals and BIGmac switches.

3. Use flashcards to support visual cues and learning.

4. Use simple language and avoid metaphors.

5. Repetition, repetition, repetition!

6. Create ritual and structure at every level and keep this consistent e.g. the structure of the session, the sequence of a music activity, the process of learning a song.

7. Use small building blocks to teach any new songs or musical material.

Singing for children with social, emotional and mental health issues[15]

Children with social, emotional and behavioural needs may be facing extremely challenging circumstances in their lives, and singing can be a chance for them to take some time out from their daily reality. It can be a good release and chance to channel some anger or emotion in a different way. It may give them an opportunity to express themselves, which could be difficult for them to do in other contexts.

Music can offer the chance to develop confidence and self-belief, as children may be able to engage with music even if they struggle in other areas of education and general life. They can also explore their own self-expression, identity and creativity, and feel a sense of control that they may not experience in other areas of their lives. Group music-making and singing can help to build social, interaction and communication skills, and children who have previously struggled to work with other people often begin to communicate and find ways to work together.

Challenges

As with all special educational needs labels, the reality for each child will be entirely individual. However, there are some common challenges particularly associated with social, emotional and behavioural needs that can cause difficulties for both the children and the teachers supporting them.

- Anxiety and feeling constantly scared or worried
- Experiencing bullying or inflicting this on others
- Difficulty forming relationships with peers and adults, and tendency to reject other people to prevent being rejected themselves
- Delayed emotional and intellectual development
- Difficulties controlling emotions and dealing with anger
- Tendency to lie
- Challenging behaviour, often in response to specific triggers

It is important to find the right ways into singing for children with social, emotional and behavioural needs. Launching straight into song learning can immediately create barriers, so it is essential to find gradual ways in that are safe, inclusive, and most importantly, fun

Activities

Warm-ups

Group warm-ups can be a great way in, and often doing these without any verbal instruction from the music leader, relying simply on copying and gesture can be really effective in creating a calm and focused atmosphere from the start. Rhythm games and pair work can be a good way to move these towards the next stages of music-making.

There are many vocal warm-ups focussing on sound effects, and exploring the voice, that allow children to have fun and explore without worrying about being 'right'. It can be helpful to try using simple graphic scores, so that children can come up with symbols to represent different ways to use their voices, and then create scores for the class to try out. You could also incorporate instruments for those children who were not ready to use their voices. You can then move onto using words and speaking in rhythm, playing with the different ways you can use your voice, such as expressing different emotions or using different accents. This can also be approached in a playful way, allowing children to gradually get rid of inhibitions and find fun and humour in using their voices.

Humming

When beginning to work with songs, humming is a great way to start learning melodies, as it can feel a lot less exposed and gives a chance for people to become confident with melodies and for a group to start to blend their voices together.

Turn-taking songs

Turn-taking songs give opportunities for individual children to have small solos, often with responses from the rest of the group. Some children may want to take time to build up their confidence to get to this point, others will want their moment to display what could be deemed as 'silly' actions or behaviour. It is worth allowing and supporting this, as long as nothing inappropriate or offensive is involved. This allows children to channel this energy into a positive activity, and to show them that their contributions are accepted and valued and allow them to enjoy the experience of the rest of the class responding.

Call and response

Call and response songs play a similar role, they can be simple and fun, and the class will learn to sing responses to the call of a leader. There can also be a movement element, which could be set, or the leader could create the movement for everyone else to copy. Children can then take on the role of the leader as they become more confident, and it is another chance to nurture a safe environment where everyone's contributions are celebrated. Another structure that can be effective is to create a call-and-response greeting song, splitting a group into two, starting with the words "Hello" on each side, and asking the children to create the rest of the singing conversation.

Build complexity

A gentle way in for older children would be to use simple songs that have potential to build up into something more complex, for example, canons, rounds and songs with layers of harmony. This would allow the music leader to teach something very simple initially, judging when the group felt completely confident having mastered this, and giving the group a sense of achievement of singing something that already sounded appealing.

Different languages

Learning songs in different languages can also provide an accessible starting point, as it can remove any barriers or associations that children may have with their use of English and language within an educational environment. It can create a chance to explore new sounds and ways to use the voice and can allow everyone to feel like they are all starting from the same point of learning, as it is likely that no-one has prior knowledge of the vocabulary. Ghanain songs can be particularly effective, as they often use sounds and syllables that are conducive to producing a strong singing sound, and they can sound immediately effective.

Different genres

If there are children in the group from different countries, you could do some research and find well-known songs from their countries and teach these to the whole group. You might also use current songs from the charts but look at different ways to arrange them with and for the group. The children can give their input and ideas on how you could sing and arrange the songs differently. Use of technology and different styles can work wonders here also, especially for those who struggle to find meaning in, or relate to, more traditional styles and repertoire. Rapping, grime, hip-hop (all with appropriate words) can be one key to unlocking engagement, confidence, creativity and a child's voice.

FINDING A POINT OF INTEREST

C showed extremely challenging behaviour in school and would often refuse to come into school at all. He was offered singing sessions and at first was not interested at all. However, when presented with a song about Minecraft his interest was sparked, and he began to engage. He began to sing songs that he liked and record himself singing. His motivation and enthusiasm increased as he began to make musical choices, evaluate his own work and begin to create an album. Teachers reported that on days when he had his singing session, he came to school willingly and was a lot calmer for the remainder of the day, His behaviour, focus, motivation and self-belief has been hugely improved through the experience.

IMPROVING UNDERSTANDING OF MUSIC

Y is three years old and nonverbal. In group sessions we worked on the singing game "Playing in a circle". Y immediately responded to the way we changed speeds and dynamics and tried to respond to this through playing instruments. After several weeks he began vocalising as well, using his voice loudly and softly, and was able to play the drums perfectly in time with the changes of speed.

INCREASING LEVELS OF ENGAGEMENT AND FOCUS

S is seven years old and on the autism spectrum. He is verbal and highly energetic and could be quite distracted and dominating in classroom situations. Through creating songs with actions in a group, he began to channel his energy and focus. At first this was by helping to make up the words and actions. As the song became familiar, he was completely engaged and concentrated on confidently singing, and leading the group in the structure of the songs by pointing at groups to take their turns in a call-and-response song. His parents told us that he began to write his own songs at home after this, finding it a positive and focussed activity.

INCREASING SELF-CONFIDENCE

Z is four years old and has learning difficulties. He was quite shy within a group and tended to copy what others around him were doing. Over several weeks of music and singing, his confidence increased and he began to take on leading roles within the small group. He enjoyed taking longer and longer solo moments within the song and shouting out and showing the signals to stop and start. He also started to initiate musical play with other children during free play times outside of the music session.

| Tip | Top Tips on social, emotional and mental health issues |

1. Find out as much as possible about the children you are working with, including any specific behaviour triggers, and adapt the way you work.

2. Be patient, approachable, calm and respectful.

3. Find out what interests them and use this to choose appropriate songs and activities.

4. Consider the set-up of the room. Some children may struggle to be in a group and may need to know that they can easily leave the room or go to a safer space if they are feeling anxious or overwhelmed.

5. Keep sessions active with lots of movement, as children may find it hard to sit still.

6. Take as many opportunities as possible to incorporate children's ideas and to celebrate their contributions, e.g. ideas for songs, how to sing or improve things.

Singing for children with sensory impairment

Singing is a different experience for a child with a visual, auditory or sensory impairment, but they gain the same pleasure from singing and music by exploring it in a suitable way for them and their needs. As a teacher, your role is to enable everyone to access singing and music with their fellow pupils; this will not look the same for every pupil you teach whether in a mainstream or SEND setting. It is important music is explored by everyone, in their own way, no matter their abilities, and who knows, maybe something musically organic may develop through giving pupils musical freedom, which may result in a new and interesting dynamic, enhancing a music session, rehearsal or performance.

Hearing impairments

It is important to remember a hearing impairment does not necessarily mean a person cannot hear any sound at all. Some hearing impairments may be specific to certain sounds and they may fluctuate throughout a person's life. It is important to remember Cochlear Implants and Hearing Aids give hearing ability, but the sounds heard can be different from the ones you are producing. Gather as much information as possible about a pupil's hearing impairment.

A hearing impairment can affect how quickly a person can recall the sounds of melodies and words. When teaching songs in any setting, it can be helpful to start with call-and-response activities line by line to ensure the melody and rhythms are correct. When working with someone with a hearing impairment, this clear repetition is a crucial step.

A hearing impairment can be one of the most isolating impairments in a music session. It's important to keep an eye on engagement levels, if pupils are lacking in responses, then try to change your approach to the session. Singing and signing is a great way to include everyone in singing activities. Signing assists recall of information and improves the understanding of words. Some pupils with learning difficulties use Makaton signing as their main form of communication, or to assist their speech so it is clearer. When teaching someone with a hearing impairment, it is important to know if they use British Sign Language or Makaton signs for consistency. You could even ask the pupil with a hearing impairment to help teach the signs to the class; a great way to encourage inclusive communication among peers.

EXPERIMENTING WITH TECHNOLOGY

D has learning difficulties and a severe hearing impairment. He is nonverbal and does not wear hearing aids. He tends to observe other pupils rather than get involved in activities himself. One day, I gave him a microphone. He shouted into the microphone at which point the entire class, also with a variety of learning difficulties, fell about laughing. The boy smiled and laughed in response to this impressive reaction from his peers and so repeated his sound. He found his voice and best of all, identified the appreciation his sounds made on his class mates.

Singing and signing

When teaching singing to pupils with various learning difficulties and disabilities, it is common for pupils to begin identifying the last word of a phrase first. You can use signing to highlight the important words you want them to focus on, and with time the small interlinking words become more apparent. Once pupils can identify signs, it's a great way of testing their memory of songs or answers to questions. You can sign phrases of songs to see if they can remember which phrase is next, or you might sing half a phrase but sign the second half to see if they can fill in the gaps. There are lots of little games and activities you can create based on this concept, a bit like *Heads, shoulders, knees and toes* and *BINGO* when sounds are gradually left out.

Signing gives nonverbal pupils a chance to join in with singing activities. However, do not let signing be their only way of joining in. Nonverbal pupils are usually happier and more engaged with an activity if they are able to play an instrument to accompany a song.

If you are not trained in a sign language, there are lots of organisations who provide online resources to learn various signs. However, there is nothing wrong with making your own signs or actions to accompany a song, as long as they are consistent. Better still, ask the pupils to choose actions. Be mindful of pupils who do use Makaton or British Sign Language as their main form of communication though, or they could get confused.

Makaton

A common communication aid is Makaton signing; used to support language. When signing Makaton, the most important words of a phrase are signed, for example, in this sentence "I am a **CHAMPION**, and **YOU'RE** gonna **HEAR** me **ROAR**", the signed words are in bold. You can simplify or increase the amount of signs based on your group.

The simplest and most common way of using Makaton is to accompany the words of songs with the gestures. This can be very effective as it supports the understanding of language within a song and allows nonverbal children to engage. This can also be supported by other staff in the classroom.

Another key way you can use Makaton is with flashcards of the symbols. They could support the learning of a song, by showing symbols for different lines of lyrics. These could be displayed whilst learning a song in short fragments, and then placed next to each other to show how the song fits together. You could also use Makaton flashcards for learning short word rhythms or sung phrases. They can be combined, reordered or duplicated to create longer phrases chosen by the children.

In groups of mixed needs and abilities you might sometimes facilitate songwriting activities using Makaton flashcards. Give small groups a selection of flashcards, each with one symbol and word written on it (e.g. friends, hello, music, together) and ask them to make some lyrics using these words, and to practise the gestures.

Makaton can also be used to conduct musical activities, e.g. by signalling a group to "stop", "sing", "stand up" and "sit down".

Makaton can give non and preverbal children a chance to participate more fully in activities and demonstrate their understanding. Using the flashcards can help with visual memory and support those with challenges in working memory, by providing an extra element and memory aid to learning activities. It can also facilitate choice and help with the understanding of musical structure.

MAKATON AND SONGS

A particularly successful example of using Makaton was using a song about the zoo with a class of nonverbal children at reception level. Each line has a Makaton gesture for an animal, which I taught the supporting staff before-hand, and the song gradually speeds up. This allowed for all of the children to be fully involved in the song, joining in the signs with the adults, and enjoying the challenge of getting faster. Children enjoyed the anticipation of trying to remember which animal was coming next.

DEVELOPING INTERACTION SKILLS AND FACILITATING

D was nonverbal and often did not seem to engage and participate in group activities, often seeming unaware of his surroundings. Through sustained engagement in singing sessions, he began to show more and more responsiveness to the group. Using Makaton flashcards to support singing and drumming rhythms, D became able to choose flashcards to determine what the group would play and sing next, showing his understanding of the cards through small vocalisations. He also increased his understanding of starting and stopping, and taking turns through songs and musical games.

> **Tip** ❯ **Top Tips on using Makaton**
>
> 1. Build songs around Makaton that are already familiar (write your own).
>
> 2. Use songs to teach new words using Makaton.
>
> 3. Teach slowly, with time to practise signs and singing, and make sure that supporting staff know the signs as well.
>
> 4. Ensure your signs are consistent and precise.
>
> 5. Highlight the key words.
>
> 6. Pupils' signing may not be as precise as yours, but do not worry about making the signing the focus of the session.

Visual impairment

A visual impairment can also be individual; colours might be more difficult or easier to see, peripheral vision may be difficult, certain lights can affect sight, a pupil might only be able to see in one direction, or out of the top of their eyes, to name a few. Reading lyrics may be a challenge, so have Braille texts ready where suitable, larger print or different coloured fonts. Within a music session, you might not change a lot for pupils with visual impairments, as singing can be learned purely through listening and mimicking the sounds around us. Pupils with visual impairments are usually very responsive to music, as they rely so much on their auditory skills to learn and understand the world. Tuning and rhythm can be a particular strength among learners with visual impairments.

Melody is usually remembered quickly, but lyrics can be tricky, particularly if a child has a learning need alongside a visual impairment. Choosing repetitive and simple songs is usually the easiest way to prevent over-complicated lyric learning and pronunciation. Echo, question-and-answer and single-phrase songs are all useful because of their simple and repetitive lyrics.

Singing can also be used to develop spatial awareness. Group singing, and musical turn-taking activities can help to get a sense of where people are in a room and can also support interaction and focus. Movement and game songs are effective, as long as all the instructions are held within the song, e.g. the lyrics tell you what and how to move. Blind young children can lack the motivation to move around, as this is usually stimulated by visual incentive, so movement songs are a good way to make movement fun and exciting and desirable. Adding in instruments, you can use songs to prompt group and solo playing, again with the instructions held within the song to avoid any need for visual or verbal cueing.

FOCUS ON AURAL LEARNING

In this setting, singing can be used as a tool to develop communication and language. Try simple songs using common every-day questions and answers, such as "How are you?" "I'm happy" which can be taught to children and then used to improvise musical dialogue. Each answer to a question is linked to a specific fragment of melody. The use of pitch can help the memory and help to develop language, as well as to develop interactive and musical skill. Children can also create their own musical questions and answers. Learning takes places by listening and copying, children can also explore the physical feelings of singing, feeling the vibrations in their lips, throat and chest.

Multi-sensory impairments

A sensory impairment can be the impairment of sight, smell, touch, taste, sound, the vestibular sense (sense of balance and spatial orientation) and proprioceptive sense (awareness of the position and movement of the body). It is important to search for more information from experts in these fields on how these sensory impairments can effect pupils and how to support them. Pupils may be hyper- or hypo-sensitive, and not adapting an environment to suit a sensory impairment can be distracting for pupils and may lead to behaviour issues, melt-downs or refusal to take part. Lights may need lowering, some children may need to run across the room every ten minutes or so; all sensory impairments are individual but pupils are still able to access singing and music.

Sound sensitivity

Try to discover which sounds they are sensitive to, usually their sensitivity is more specific than "they don't like loud sounds". You might teach children who wear ear defenders but will hit a gong as loud as they can! Narrowing down the sounds a pupil finds difficult can improve their tolerance of sound.

Vestibular and proprioceptive

Running and jumping around the room can seem disruptive, but you can get some lovely responses from pupils who are allowed to move as they wish. Try to ensure the room is set up appropriately for them so as not to distract everyone else. Have confidence, just because they don't look engaged does not mean their movement is not helping them take it all in.

If pupils have more than one impairment, be creative in how they can access music. Touch, music and movement, vibrations, large bass speakers, music-responsive lights, live music, recorded music, visual music apps, headphones, sensory set-ups, thematic set-ups, all aid access to music. Be creative to discover what music looks, feels, sounds, tastes and smells like to them.

> **ENGAGING SENSES**
>
> M is a pupil with severe autism, he doesn't like wearing shoes, is visually impaired, is nonverbal and walks around the room constantly. One day he walked around the room which was set up like Antarctica, the walls were draped with white fabric, blue crunchy tarpaulin on the floor, ice blocks, shiny things, bells and twinkly chimes. While the class beat a rhythm together, the pupil approached a drum at the opposite side of the room and beat it perfectly in time. This pupil now interacts with others through music and singing, especially when all his senses are engaged.

Singing and making music for children with physical impairments

Children's physical disabilities can be very varied, but one of the best things about music is the variety of possible activities and resources that are available to us as teachers. You can find all sorts of ways of supporting pupils in their music making, regardless of their physical disabilities:

- Large gathering drums can be angled for pupils to kick
- Resonance boards can be used for pupils to lie on
- Blowing whistles and recorders can encourage mouth motor skills
- Phonetic sounds can be practised through singing
- Big beaters and small beaters with different handles (or anything a pupil can grasp easily) can be used to hit a drum. Egg shakers are also easy to hold
- Microphones and loop systems can pick up any sound and turn them into musical phrases
- Drums can be placed on tilted stands to reach wheelchair height
- A pupil's fingers can be rested on a harp or guitar and allow the hand to fall down the strings to produce sound
- Chimes can create a big sound with only very little movement

The biggest challenge when working with pupils with physical disabilities is deciding how much physical support to provide. Well-intended staff and other pupils can have a tendency to hold the limbs of those with physical disabilities to give them more movement. But any movement the pupil can manage by themselves to create sound will be more rewarding.

Using tablets – like iPads – can be very helpful, particularly when working with children with very limited movement. Apps like Thumbjam and Garageband allow you to record pupils' vocalisations and turn them into 'instruments' which they can 'play' with very small finger movements. In addition, something like a Wowee speaker, which turns any surface into sound, makes an ideal tactile sensory addition to the music-making experience.

INDEPENDENCE AND CONTROL

I learned an excellent technique at the beginning of my career in some training with Jessie's Fund; they suggested we lift and drop the arm of pupils with profound physical needs onto a drum, this way the pupil is making the sound and better still, the pupil is gaining an awareness of the motion and the muscles they might need to make the gesture themselves. Since this training, I have found all sorts of different ways of giving pupils with physical disabilities the chance to make sounds independently. I prefer pupils to independently make a sound here and there throughout a session, rather than hear the sound of an able bodied adult holding a child's hand with a beater in it hitting a drum in time. At least this way, the pupil is the one in control; a rarity for pupils with physical disabilities.

Emily Tully, SEND Music and Singing Teacher

Allow lots of time for those with physical disabilities to respond. If pupils are able to communicate verbally, you can try to include a singing section in an activity, as this is usually the easiest way for them to make music. Let pupils lead a group activity with the beat of a drum; find ways of making their small sounds and movements part of a larger musical picture. Think about how you can provide opportunities for small steps of fine and gross motor skill development. Try setting realistic goals for pupils that can help them to develop muscular and physical responses and lead to better motor skills being acquired over time.

When working with pupils with physical disabilities, it is easier to see and imagine how the disability affects the pupil more than any other disability. For example, if a pupil can hold a beater but can't grasp tightly and it falls out, try this action yourself and how it feels; put yourself in the pupil's physical position and see how you might help them overcome it. Give pupils lots of options, try lots of different instruments and see if some actions are easier for them than others. For children who are cognitively able, be tactful in how you aid them and how it looks in front of their peers, try not to focus on adaptation so much that they feel singled out.

> **Tip** ▶ **Top Tips on singing for children with physical impairments**
>
> 1. Be creative – how can they access this instrument?
>
> 2. Use technology – iPads, Skoog, Soundbeam etc. to enable learners to access sound and music. You could also try using adapted instruments – OHMI (One Handed Musical Instrument Trust) for example. Also microphones with echo or reverb/effects and looper pedals can be used to enhance and record vocal responses. Adjustable microphone stands are also useful to have to hand.
>
> 3. Get pupils out of chairs where possible – if pupils have medical or toileting needs, discuss this with professionals to see if it can be changed so the pupil can come out of their chair in music.
>
> 4. Don't over-support with physical prompts.
>
> 5. Allow small but independent responses.
>
> 6. Look for small steps of progress, they could grow into something much bigger.
>
> 7. Allow lots of time – don't be afraid of silences... they are where the magic can happen.

Overall

Be aware of impairments but do not allow them to be the focus of a session. When it comes to inclusivity, what better way to include everyone in an activity than through singing together? Those with visual impairments naturally learn audibly, those with sensory impairments find comfort in the predictability and pattern of music, and those with hearing impairments can see they are part of the group. Singing can demonstrate a pupil's highest level of musical awareness and ability. They do not need to learn how to play an instrument; singing is natural and although pupils may find communicating in the "usual" way difficult, they have practised communicating all their life, it is their greatest skill. Singing gives opportunities to respond organically to music, building on the skills we already have.

LEVEL PLAYING FIELD

Singing puts everyone on a level playing field. It is very rewarding as a teacher to see those with various learning needs and impairments become assimilated among mainstream choirs; pupil's faces have lit up as their rehearsed music suddenly surrounds them with a greater impact, and they feel a part of something special.

Tip	Top Tips on singing with SEND children

1. Keep going – you don't know how much is being understood and taken in sometimes, one day you might get a response that astounds you.

2. Inclusivity – make sessions inclusive by giving everyone an opportunity to join in, do solos or lead sessions.

3. Where possible, find some time to work one-to-one with pupils who have the most severe disabilities. Allow sessions to be pupil-led so you can discover new things about their musical abilities.

4. Become a natural – the more you develop your teaching and adaptation to individual pupils, the easier it will get. Really focus on their needs at the start of the year, and soon, you will naturally adapt sessions to suit them without even thinking about it.

5. Be creative – try new things, do things differently and allow pupils space to improvise or have an input. Let them lead you and remember, music is expressive.

6. Use technology where appropriate and where possible to amplify or put effects on voices. This can motivate and encourage those who are not always confident vocally and can also reinforce the sense of 'self' and 'other'. Remember to position the speakers close to learners so they can hear themselves.

7. Explore as many different styles and types of repertoire as you can in sessions – have a go at recreating these styles together.

8. Live performances – book practitioners or run school trips where pupils can see, hear and feel music with different perspectives. Live orchestra trips can trigger some incredible responses from pupils.

7

TEACHING MUSIC THROUGH SINGING

In this chapter, we are going to look at the role singing can play in helping pupils to learn music and develop as musicians. The voice is our first instrument, it is inside us and helps us experience music from the inside out. It connects the musical computer, our brain, with our voice and ear.

Of course, singing doesn't require any expensive instruments because everyone already has a voice. Remember, singing need not just be about warming up or performing. It can be the basis for improvising, arranging and composing and it can be used to explore instrumental music and support instrumental learning.

When we sing, we are literally embodying music, which helps to embed theoretical concepts as physical experiences, making them easier to understand, remember and reproduce. Questions of texture, timbre, rhythmic vocabulary, pitch and musical notation can be investigated and then understood through the process of singing, with pupils learning to internalise musical concepts through the experience of producing and controlling their own sound. There is a long tradition of using movement to underpin musical learning, for example, through the Dalcroze and Kodály methods, which in their different ways use body and voice to develop musical knowledge and understanding.

Singing is also an excellent route into developing musicianship skills. It is an ingrained part of early child development in most cultures around the world. Parents singing with their babies and young children is a form of language development and parent-child bonding. Building on this natural inclination will help children to develop aural skills from an early age, such as the ability to recognise changes in pitch and pitch-match with the voice, and rhythmic decoding – the ability to listen to and copy rhythmic patterns. This, in turn, is part of developing musical memory, and pattern and structure recognition.

Regular singing will:

- Improve listening skills and support pupils to identify differences in pitch and rhythm
- Develop musical memory leading to more effective singing and playing from memory
- Improve interval recognition and being able to sing them – an important step towards learning to read and sight-sing notation
- Help internalise melodic and harmonic material encouraging older students to identify chords, cadences and modulations

- Improve accurate pitching
- Develop singing in harmony
- Help learn how to phrase music – linked to breath
- Develop ensemble skills – by listening to those around them when they are singing.

Kodály

In the 1930s, the Hungarian composer Zoltán Kodály advocated a child-centred approach that placed singing at the heart of all musical learning.[16] Using games and activities that follow on from children's instinctive play, Kodály combined simple rhythm names (such as 'ta' and 'ti-ti') and a series of hand signs and solfa ('do, re, mi…') to create a structure for learning to read musical notation. These powerful tools, involving the whole body in learning, develop recall and musical memory and are used during singing exercises.

Kodály-based classes are founded on creating a strong sense of play, teamed with structured musical learning. Moving swiftly between different songs and activities, you can cover an extraordinary range of musical learning in a 30-minute lesson, using singing to teach musical principles, including pitch, pulse and rhythmic notation. Here are some example activities, for each one there are suggested songs to use from the Sing Up Song Bank:

Find the pulse	Song Bank suggestions
(Developing pulse)	
Sing a familiar song and invite every child to mark the pulse in whichever way they choose: tapping the head, marching on the spot, patting the stomach - the more playful the better!	The animal fair The grand old Duke of York

Pass the pulse	Song Bank suggestions
(Developing pulse)	
Take a familiar, steady-paced song, stand in a circle, and ask the children to pass a steady clap one-by-one around the circle as they sing. To make the exercise more challenging, try this activity while singing a song with a variable speed. Don't worry if it takes a few goes, and notice that the next child in the circle can help stabilise the pulse if it wobbles every now and then.	Roll the old chariot along Who stole my chickens and my hens? More challenging: Five fine bumble bees Kalinka

Musical pencils

(Pitch awareness)

Build your pupils' awareness of pitch through the idea of musical pencils. Before beginning a song, ask the children to conjure up an imaginary musical pencil and then to 'draw' the shape of the melody as they sing. These shapes help children gain a practical sense of how musical pitch rises and falls, also connecting pitch to the physical sensation of singing the different tones.

Song Bank suggestions

A little echo

Up and down

Melody cards

(Pitch awareness)

Draw the shape of a melody in graphic symbols. Ask questions like: How many notes are there? How many *different* notes are there? Draw each phrase then sing together following the shape. You can turn them into graphic cards like these:

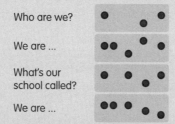

Who are we?

We are ...

What's our school called?

We are ...

Set groups the challenge of working out the next phrase of the tune, firstly using the imaginary pencil and then matching it with its corresponding graphic representation. Ask questions like: Is the second phrase the same as the first? What clues will help us work this out?

Song Bank suggestions

Who are we?

Echo songs

(Musical memory)

Echo songs (where the response is a melodic echo of the call) are a good way of attuning the ear. Not only does this type of song require the 'responding' singers to match the pitch of the 'caller,' it also means that singers have to listen carefully to the melody, rhythm and words and recall them, developing musical memory. Songs that enable you to insert words relevant to your class are particularly effective, e.g. 'Who are we? [echo] We are class seven! [echo]'.

Song Bank suggestions

Boom chicka boom

Copy kitten

Tongo

The voice in our heads

(Inner hearing)

Singing also supports the development of what Kodály refers to as 'inner hearing' or our 'thinking voice'. This idea of inner hearing is the ability to hear music inside our heads without needing to play an instrument or sing. It helps us sing and play in tune, to make music sensitively and responsively with others, and to read and eventually sight-sing notation.

In BINGO, try singing one of the letters in your head rather than out loud (starting with 'B').

Song Bank suggestions

Baby one, two, three

BINGO

Rounds

(Inner hearing)

Rounds require pupils to listen, sing and adjust their sound simultaneously to become part of an ensemble.

Song Bank suggestions

Janie Mama

Shoes of shining leather

Si si si

Melody staircase

(Pitch awareness)

To help your pupils work out the notes of the song, draw a staircase on the board with six stairs. Pick a note to represent number one (C is good) and sing the numbers from one up to six. Do this several times up and down to get a sense of the pitch. On which step does your song start? Where does it go next? How many steps up/down?

Song Bank suggestions

1, 121

Janie Mama

Shoes of shining leather

Si si si

Dalcroze

Émile Jaques-Dalcroze (1865–1950) was a Swiss composer, pianist and teacher of harmony who took a particular interest in the fact that his students lacked a sense of 'inner hearing', rhythmic accuracy and expression in performance. He believed that the body should be prepared for music-making, through physical engagement with rhythm and aural and vocal engagement with sound, before playing an instrument. His method is known as 'Dalcroze Eurhythmics', which means 'good flow'. Today, it's referred to as simply 'Dalcroze'.

Today, Dalcroze lessons ideally happen in a large space, where the class is free to express itself. Music is experienced before it is discussed. For example, 'the black notes with sticks' (crotchets) will have been felt as marching music and 'the white notes without sticks' (semibreves) will have been introduced as 'moon walks' much later, and in relation to the marching beat. This body knowledge is absorbed before the written symbol is shown. Every aspect of what we think of as music theory is taught in this active, creative way.

During teacher training, the emphasis is on the 'doing', in order to gain an experience and understanding of the principles that underpin the method. This encourages teachers to invent exercises of their own, which nourishes their creativity. And it means that you will never run out of ideas!

Here are some activities based on the Dalcroze approach, suggestions of songs to use from the Song Bank have been given for each one.

> "When you're singing, your body is the instrument. Everything is connected, especially the ears: you can't help but engage deeply with music."
>
> Katherine Zeserson, musician

Get a move on
(Pulse and subdivisions)
Songs that have a steady walking pulse are excellent for externalising a pulse that is felt on the inside. Move to the pulse in any number of ways: either stepping in and out of a circle together, stepping round in a circle and changing direction at the end of each line, body patching (patting either the left, right or both thighs with hands), or use creative ideas from the children. These actions can be done twice as fast at a given signal, or twice as slowly at another signal, so that the relationships between note values are understood (quavers, crotchets, minims).

Song Bank suggestions

Building

In the autumn

Human machine

(Pulse and subdivisions)
In groups of three, each child takes a different note value and invents a repetitive action for it, for example, quaver is a hand-wave, crotchet is one hand on your head and minim is holding both arms out to the side of your body. When put together, the actions form a human machine, showing rhythmic relationships (a song backing track can be played as they work on this).

Song Bank suggestions

On my way

We will rock you

Head, shoulders, knees and toes

(Physical awareness and pulse)
Young children need to learn about the geography of their bodies. Head, shoulders, knees and toes is a perennial favourite, but by improvising on its structure, by children suggesting alternative body parts, the song is ever-new. Coordination, memory and sequencing abilities are also developed in the process.

Song Bank suggestions

Head, shoulders, knees and toes

The train line

(Musical cues and quick reaction)
The train line game can be played whilst singing *Train coming*, or whilst the song is being played. The children form a 'train line', one behind the other (or a few smaller trains), and they move along to the beat of the song. The teacher chooses two musical signals – either two contrasting percussion instruments or two notes on the piano. One signal indicates that everyone jumps to face the other way, and the other indicates that the leader goes to the back of the line. This game can be made as easy or as challenging as is age-appropriate. Simply moving in the space, developing spatial awareness, stopping and starting, gathering pace and slowing down will be enough of a challenge for younger ones, whilst older children will enjoy the challenge of the mixed signals and cooperating as a team.

Song Bank suggestions

Train coming

Work songs

(Equipment)

Moving the stones on the Song Bank is written in the style of a work song, where repetitive rhythms are sung by groups of workers as a way of keeping up morale and maintaining a steady working rhythm.

Here is an idea involving the use of equipment. In a Dalcroze class, equipment is used to give the body experience of a movement quality, such as 'rebound' from a ball (bouncing it on the beat and learning appropriate dosage of energy), and lightness and flow from a scarf (for understanding musical line and phrase). Beanbags are very useful for instilling a sense of pulse in the body. By learning to pass them round the circle whilst singing, the children are also improving their coordination, lateralisation (localisation of function on either the right or left sides of the brain) and teamwork skills. Start by getting the action going first (correct hand and direction) before introducing a few beanbags at a time.

Song Bank suggestions

Moving the stones

Wonky beats

(Metre)

Songs from other countries often give us an opportunity to get a feeling for different metres. *Thalasa*, from Greece, is an example of this. The song has an 'unequal beat' (written in 7/8). It starts with a swaying beat, followed by two marching beats. In a circle, start by getting the class to sway from side to side then to contrast this with marching on the spot. Try various combinations before you fix on one sway and two marches – one compound and two simple-time beats. See if they can maintain this whilst singing the song.

Song Bank suggestions

Thalasa

Learning to read and write... music

Music is a language, and like any language, if you are immersed in it when you're young, it really isn't that tricky to learn to read, write and understand it. It's actually very logical, and more consistent than other languages. The opportunity to be immersed in music however is normally only available to a minority of children. By creating a culture of singing in your school, every child is given a medium with which to learn the language of music, and given the best opportunity to fulfil their potential as musicians. There are, of course, eminent musicians who don't read music, and whole genres of music which are based around the aural tradition and improvisation. However, becoming fluent can provide a springboard to broader and deeper engagement with different types of music and enable you to accurately communicate your own musical ideas to other musicians so they can be performed. Learning the basics of reading and writing notated music will open up a well-rounded music education and greater options to pupils later in life.

We should remember that learning to read and write words takes significant time and concentrated effort. Throughout this process we encourage children to play games with sounds, create words and then sentences, tell stories, chant poems and express themselves – using their limited reading and writing skills in motivating, purposeful ways that make sense to them. Gradually children are able to encode (write) and decode (read), using symbols that can be combined in infinite ways. We have realistic expectations that their spoken use of language will be far superior to their reading and writing of coded cues to begin with.

What would it be like if we followed the same principles with musical notation? By encouraging their ability to express music and to think in music first and then using creative means to connect the sounds with the symbols, while recognising that children's use of notations will typically lag far behind. Reading and writing music notation opens doors in the musical world just as reading and writing words opens up the literary world. Singing is the ideal medium for children to begin to connect the dots on the page with the sounds they are producing.

Sound before symbol

'Sound before symbol' is often deemed a desirable approach to musical learning, and there is little merit in teaching notation away from music-making as this negates the interdependent relationship between sounds and symbols. In his book, *The Sounding Symbol: Music Education in Action* (Nelson Thornes, 1995), George Odam argues that the symbols must not 'get in the way of the sounds they represent' and that 'thinking in sound, imagining sound, constructing possible sounds in the head and improvising music all have to be established as skills before the symbols for these things are learned'. This point of view proposes that practical musical activity should be the focus of music education, from which purposeful use of notations can develop.

It is important to note the plural term 'notations' – the idea that multiple notation systems should be considered. 'Tablature' (Tab for short) is effective for showing ukulele and guitar chords. It provides a visual representation of the fingerboard and is often used alongside staff notation. There is plenty of repertoire in the Sing Up Song Bank based around a limited number of chords, and children may use these chords to create their own songs. Tab notation therefore has a specific purpose in this case.

Song Bank Playlist: Songs with max 4 chords
Janie mama (F, Gm, C)
Jamawaile (D, Bm)
Mash it up (D, A, Bm, G)
Nanuma (C, Dm7)
Reggae riffs (D, A, Bm, G)
Three little birds (D, A, G)

Symbols can be used with young children to support and extend musical learning. One way to approach this may be to use physical objects to represent a sound, pattern of sounds or a stave. From this starting point, graphic notation can be introduced.

In graphic notation, begin with showing melody rising and falling more generally, rather than precise pitches. The best way to get started is to allow the pupils to invent their own music and then discover that in order to remember what happens when, and be able to make the same music again on another day, it helps to write something down as a memory-jogger. It will also help them to explain what their musical idea is, if they want to include a new pupil in their musical group. Quite often, when children make up their own music they may use 'invented' notation systems, drawing, in part, on something they already know.

Relating sound to symbol

Initially, it is essential for children to understand the relationship between sounds, silence and symbols. Voice work is very useful for this. For example, ask children to hold up different colours on card. Taking the children's suggestions, assign one vocal sound to each symbol, e.g. a telephone ring for square and a cuckoo for circle. As the 'conductor' points to a symbol, the class should make the assigned sound.

telephone ring   cuckoo

There are many ways you could develop this musical game. The children could work in groups to create their own pieces based on two sounds and then notate them with colours or shapes (encoding). They could 'read' left to right from a score of the two colours or shapes (decoding) to perform the music. You could explicitly introduce silence, different pitches (depending on how high up the colours / shapes are placed) and volume (perhaps using different sizes of paper).

In standard (staff) notation, pitch and rhythm are different yet interrelated aspects needing careful consideration. In terms of pitch, we need to instil an understanding that the pitch of a note (how high or low the note is and which direction the music is moving in) is related to its vertical position.

The game *Stairs and Elevators* is useful for this. As the teacher's hands move up by step, the giant walks up the stairs and the children's voices go up the scale. If the giant takes the elevator up, the hands and voices slide (the musical term for this is *glissando*) upwards from low to high. The giant can also come down the stairs or the elevator.

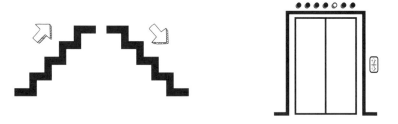

Once children are familiar with this game, it can be adapted in multiple ways. For example, half the class can follow the conductor's directions while the other half show with their hands or notate what they hear with their backs to the conductor. Children could compose and notate their own short 'stairs and elevator' pieces and have others play the piece from the notation. This leads into the idea of jumping from a low step to a high step and the pitch of the notes being further apart. What would this sound like? What would it look like? Such games offer a simple way into reading and writing graphic scores.

Song Bank playlist: 2- or 3-note songs

Copy kitten (2 notes)

Hey, hey (2 notes)

Hi lo, chicka lo (3 notes)

Ring a ring o' roses (3 notes)

Step back baby (3 notes)

Witch, witch (3 notes)

Introducing only two notes on staff notation, at least in the first instance, is another useful strategy. Using the notes G and E you can teach a lot of songs and games, get children to invent their own and also establish an understanding of 'lines and spaces' in relation to the staff. It can also make it easier to teach pitch and rhythm together.

STARTING AND DEVELOPING CHOIRS

A Singing School includes every child, and embeds singing into the very fabric of the school, across multiple settings and contexts. One of the best contexts for children to experience singing and for your school to exhibit the singing you are doing, is a choir.

In this chapter, we are going to think about what makes a school choir (they come in all different shapes and sizes), what types of choirs would be best-suited to the school community you serve, what contribution they might make to school life and to your vision of being a Singing School, and finally, how to get started and develop your choirs.

What makes a choir?

Your choir will be as inclusive as possible and a positive, encouraging experience for every child. Singing together in a school choir should be a joyful experience – a moment of bonding and togetherness for the singers without the pressures of individual academic targets. Taking part in group singing can help children learn to express themselves, build friendships and develop their social skills. Choral singing in its essence should be about "how good can we sound together?" and the joy of being part of that group experience and endeavour. As the leader of the choir, you will set the tone and the culture of the group's behaviour and experience. If you are enthusiastic and joyful in your approach, your pupils will be too.

Singing in a choir can be both enjoyable and hard work. Indeed, working hard together as a team on improving how the choir sounds is the reward and the joy of being part of it. Children are discerning adjudicators of quality and of progress being made (or not!) and they will invariably spot when something they are part of is not up to scratch. So, you don't need to worry about setting them stretching but achievable targets – just as you would in the classroom. Furthermore, because it is a group, rather than an individual, endeavour, everyone contributes – stronger and weaker singers alike – and all gain the same feeling of satisfaction and reward from the group's achievements. You will also find that the weaker singers will be able to sing much better when singing among stronger singers. So much of singing in a choir is about listening to those around you and mimicking the sound they are making in order to achieve a good overall blended sound. If those around you are making a wonderful sound, you can't help but be improved by that yourself.

Tip >> **Spread the sound around**

Intersperse your less experienced singers with some of your more confident and capable singers, you'll be amazed at the positive effect it has on the overall sound.

By aiming for your choir rehearsals to be enjoyable and inclusive, you are not giving up on quality singing or on achievements being made – quite the contrary, in fact.

Types of choir

Within your school you may want to consider a range of options for different types of choirs. You might want to create class choirs, choirs for particular year-groups or key-stages, whole-school choirs, staff choirs, parents or community choirs, boys or girls only, small groups, large groups, genre-specific choirs, e.g. gospel, rock, show-choirs. You might also be thinking about ability level and building in some progression, for example, you might have an all-comers choir plus an auditioned choir, or a chamber choir for your older and most able singers.

Then, you'll want to think about how your choir(s) will learn repertoire – by ear, by reading notation, or a bit of both. And how much repertoire you want to sing with accompaniment, how much *a cappella*. You might want to set up a specific *a cappella* group.

What will your choir(s) be working towards? Do you want to work towards a performance? If so, how formal will the performance be? You might want to keep your choir to be mainly 'for fun' or you might want to get really serious about it and enter choral competitions.

Starting a choir

If there is no existing culture or tradition of singing in your school, it can seem daunting to set up a choir and even more so to keep one going. Start by enthusing about your new choir venture. Talk to everyone in the school about it as often as you can and exude enthusiasm and excitement about the project – it will be contagious.

Making plans

Firstly, you will want to work out when the best times and days of the week for choir rehearsals are. You want to avoid pupils needing to be absent from other lessons or activities in order to attend choir – particularly if you want it to be as inclusive as possible.

Consult school staff and pupils to see what type of singing they would like to be happening in school and factor their aspirations into your plans.

Find a space to practise where there is plenty of space, light and air, and where it is relatively quiet. You will need the space for warm-ups, if it is light and airy it will be a healthier environment in which to sing, and you want it to be quiet so there aren't too many distractions, and you are not straining to be heard above extraneous noise. Make sure the room isn't too hot. Standing up for an extended period and singing while too hot can lead to pupils fainting! Keep the room well ventilated, allow jumpers and jackets to be removed, and encourage drinking water. Spend some rehearsal time sitting (on chairs not on the floor), if it is too long for the children to stand. But remind them to maintain good posture while they are singing, even when they are seated.

To kick things off, you might want to arrange a big singing event, where the whole school gets involved in some singing on one day – you could use Sing Up Day. Having one big singing event will generate interest and enthusiasm for your project and help you to publicise it across the whole school. Use this opportunity to recruit pupils for the choir. Ask them to sign up, give them letters to take home, get the rest of the staff on-board so they can also encourage their pupils to get involved.

Fix a schedule of regular rehearsals, so everyone knows when and where they will take place and then you can begin to prepare your song and warm-up selection and get ready for the first session.

Sing Up Day is one day each year when schools and singing groups from all over the world join together to sing a specially-composed Sing Up song to celebrate the power of collective singing.

Choosing appropriate songs

To begin with, choose songs that you are familiar with, or can learn easily and which you are enthusiastic about. Your enthusiasm and confidence with the song will rub off on your pupils.

Consult the pupils. Find out what style of singing they would like to do and what songs they would like to sing. Do they have any aspirations to sing in an assembly or a concert? Do some of them already sing regularly outside of school? Keep on consulting them and engaging them in discussion about how the choir should progress as you go, this will help you to do a better job for them and give them more say in their own progress.

Blend their song choices with your own so you can achieve balance and expand their musical horizons. You may be surprised at how open young children are to trying out lots of different styles of music outside of what they already know from radio, TV and films. Try some songs from other world cultures – traditional folk songs, as well as a range of pop, gospel and classical styles. And to keep the boys engaged, make sure you aren't singing only songs by female pop artists. Ask the boys to make song suggestions and keep their possible male singing role models in mind too.

Choose something that is relatively simple and achievable to begin with. Once you have got the choir up and running, you can gradually include more stretching choices that will challenge them. You will get to know what is easy for them, what is too hard and what is just the right amount of challenge. It is good to set aspirations high, but achievable. Sounding good early on is an excellent motivator and is related to the material you choose to sing.

Complexities in songs that you should watch out for include:

Vocal range

Listen to the children's voices for signs of them straining to reach the notes. Does the song go too high or too low for the voices at any point? It may be that a bit of quick re-arranging of the tune can solve this, or you may be able to split your singers so that those who can reach the high or low notes do so, while the others sing an alternative line. There are no hard and fast rules except not to make young voices sing beyond a range that is comfortable for them. It won't sound good and their voices will get tired.

> **Tip** ❯ **Tailor the song to fit the voices**
>
> If the song is in the wrong key for your singers, try starting on a different starting note. Move up or down one note at a time until you find the key that sits comfortably. Usually you won't need to adjust by more than one tone.
>
> If by doing this, you find that other sections become out of range at the opposite end of the spectrum, the overall range may be too wide. In which case, re-arrange the melody to narrow the range, or switch songs.

Tessitura

This relates to whether long passages of a song are on the high-side or on the low-side. Voices can often manage the odd high or low note, but long passages which are outside their comfortable range will put strain on the voice. You will be able to hear the voices tiring if this is the case. You could just choose a different song or you could adjust the key of the song (transposition). Unaccompanied songs can be transposed into a more comfortable key by using a different starting note. If you have a piano accompanist, they may be willing and able to transpose the accompaniment but don't just assume they can – it is quite an advanced skill. Some notation software or digital sheet music retailers allow you to select the key you want the notation in. And some backing tracks can be transposed through use of software too.

Speed

You will need to think about speed of notes and speed of lyrics. Slowing them down while learning the song might solve it, but younger children will struggle with lots of very fast words.

Appropriateness of lyrics

This can be surprisingly difficult, particularly if you are inviting the children to request their favourite pop songs. Many are fine, but some are not. At Sing Up, our general rule is to imagine young children singing the song to a hall full of parents and teachers, and decide whether that would feel comfortable or not. Sometimes it is the implied subject matter or the connotation rather than the lyrics themselves that are the problem. It's subjective of course, but at Sing Up we avoid anything connected with sex, swearing, violence, alcohol and drugs. Even then there are grey areas – love songs, even sea shanties (*What shall we do with the drunken sailor* is probably OK!), and folk songs – all can have content that feels inappropriate. Use your judgement according to what feels right for the age-group you are working with and the culture of your school.

Vocal and musical complexity

- **Singing in unison or in parts** is your first choice to make. You will want to begin with unison songs with inexperienced singers, getting them to listen well to each other when they are singing and making a nice, blended unison sound. As they progress you can move on to rounds and canons to get them used to holding separate parts. Then you can move on to some simple part-singing, gradually building up layers of complexity and difficulty as you go.
- **Breath control** is something singers acquire as they get more advanced and physically bigger. When they are young they will struggle with singing very long phrases and will need to breathe more frequently than older singers.
- **Singing melodies that move by step** or with jumps of small intervals are simpler than melodies with big jumps. If the song you want to sing has some big jumps in it, practise these first. Get the children to listen to the melody and help them to learn to pitch the jump by hearing it in their heads before they try to sing it.
- **Vocal agility** is something that develops over time. In the same way that you wouldn't expect a young child who has just mastered a forward roll to immediately be able to do a complex gymnastics routine, the voice becomes more agile and able to tackle complex melodic patterns with time and practice.

Leading rehearsals

What is the purpose of rehearsals? It isn't just about learning repertoire and singing songs over and over again, it is about improving something and working towards a goal. It helps if you first unpick exactly what you are trying to achieve and then break it down into manageable chunks to be spread across a number of weeks, ensuring that you can cover all the repertoire in the given time.

It is also helpful to break the work down per rehearsal session and to remember that you don't have to tackle everything at once.

The balance and pace of your rehearsal sessions will make or break whether pupils enjoy coming to choir. So, think about this carefully and be alert to how the group is responding. A good rehearsal will include:

- a warm-up
- some challenges or difficult sections
- something familiar
- a straight performance or run-through of something.

This will mean that there is a good balance of hard work and satisfying singing. The experience will be a combination of shared hard work, listening and reflecting on the sound being made, lots of fun and should leave pupils with a sense of achievement and wanting to come back for more.

As with other singing contexts we've already discussed, the setting and space you rehearse in is a crucial element. You need a nice light, open and airy space with plenty of room and no distractions. Pupils need to be able to see you and any audio equipment or piano needs to be close to hand. Depending on the size of your group, rows of semi-circled chairs is ideal, although sometimes you might want to work in a circle, especially if you are learning music by ear. Experiment with this and see what produces the best results in terms of everyone being able to hear each other and listen really well to the sound being produced. If you have a very large number of singers en masse, like the whole school, you could try organising each class sitting around the outside of the hall facing inwards and have the singing leader in the middle. The beauty of this is everyone can see the leader and each other.

Organising voices

There are a variety of ways to do this, but if you are working mostly in unison, having a critical mass in the centre of your choir with your strongest singers in the middle can be effective. Alternatively, dotting these singers around the space will help spread the sound to the less confident singers and improve tone and blend. Generally, you will want to group voices that are singing the same part together so that they can hear and support each other, but once the parts are secure and well-learnt it can be incredibly useful to mix everyone up so that they have to hold their part on their own and listen to the other parts around them. This will help develop a much stronger sense of what is happening in the music and better ensemble overall.

Seated or standing

An ideal rehearsal will involve both. You won't want your singers standing for a whole rehearsal, particularly if they are very young, but equally the sound will improve if they are standing up. You can use this to give the singing a boost at particular moments. If you sense that energy and focus is flagging, or if it would help to convey a particular vocal technique to be standing, take particular moments to stand up and get an instant lift to the sound and concentration. It's also helpful to have your choir standing for the performance moments of a rehearsal.

Learning the material

It is often useful to do the hardest material at the start after you have warmed up. Then the session gets easier after that. Break things into chunks and employ a range of tactics such as speaking the words, clapping the rhythms, working on diction or pronunciation or humming the tune to focus your singers on particular areas and embed the learning you are aiming for. Putting your singers in the role of listeners is also useful. To do this, you can have half the group sing while the other half listens and feeds back. At the same time, don't be afraid to park and come back to things that pupils are struggling with, sometimes doing something different for a short while and then returning to the tricky part can bring a freshness to the challenge and make it easier to overcome. Avoid singing with your pupils all the time because it makes them rely on following your voice and makes it harder for you to be listening to them. Better to sing phrases to them and then have them echo what they have heard while you listen.

Length of session

For a primary-aged choir, anywhere between 20 and 45 minutes is ideal. Longer than that and you might need to build in some down time, as well as toilet and drink breaks.

Accompaniment

Whether you are working with live or recorded accompaniment, you will need to practise with and without it in rehearsal and make sure that the balance between the voices and the accompaniment is at the right level. Your singers will need to be able to hear the accompaniment clearly in order to keep in time and in tune with it, but they also should not feel they need to strain their voices to be heard over it. If you can possibly find a way for them to sing some repertoire with live accompaniment, it will be a very positive experience and an important one for the development of their musicianship and ensemble skills.

Perfecting and polishing

Having a performance goal to work towards is a great motivator for some hard work on the final polishing and perfecting of a song. The same rule about not always beginning at bar 1 applies to this stage too. Starting your rehearsal at different parts of the song will ensure that you don't end up with the first section of the song being terrific, and then gradually tailing off as it becomes less secure. Some focussed work on a tricky section that needs more attention will pay dividends later.

Memorising

Think about whether you want the choir to sing from memory or not. You will get a better performance from them if you can get them to memorise everything. You will have their full attention, rather than them looking at sheets of lyrics or whiteboards, and they will be in a much better position to make sure that the performance really connects with the audience.

Meaning

Get them to think about the meaning of the words. If they've been learning the song for a while the words may well be on auto-pilot by now and have lost all sense of meaning. Remind them that a big part of performing is to communicate what the song is about to the audience. So, they need to think about how to do that through the way they sing each phrase, the expression that goes into it, the dynamics and phrasing, as well as their facial expressions and any actions you have decided to incorporate.

Enunciating

Remind them that the words need to be clearly heard – no mumbling. Clear, crisp consonants that are placed precisely so everyone enunciates them at the same time together with nice open vowel sounds will help to achieve this clarity. Watch out that you don't overdo it however, particularly for styles of music where a more relaxed approach to enunciating the words is more appropriate. Nothing sounds more comical than a choir singing a rock anthem with perfectly enunciated words.

Tidying up

Then there will be some general tidying up and tightening of particular sections and corners you might want to do. Beginnings and endings, plus any transitions from one section to another often need this kind of attention, particularly if there is a key-change or a change of tempo. There will be tricky moments unique to each song that you will already know about that need ironing out and practising until they are as good as the rest of the song. You will want to check on tuning, rhythmic accuracy and 'togetherness' – is the choir singing as one?

Tone and blend

Make sure no voices are sticking out and work on tonal quality. If you are singing songs in parts, check for balance between them and ask your singers to listen out for this too – it isn't a competition between the parts. They need to take responsibility for blending and balancing their voices by listening to each other. Generally, the melody should be slightly louder than the other parts and you will need to point out which part has the melody as it may move around from one part to another.

Start together

Are you using a backing track? If so, get really familiar with it and make sure you know where to bring everyone in.

What approach are you going to take to starting songs without backing tracks? If you are going to use hand gestures, have you practised in the mirror? Have you tried it out with others to make sure they understand your musical intentions?

> **Tip** >> **How do we sound?**
>
> **Use the checklist of reflective statements below to get your singers doing the hard work of listening to and critiquing their own performance.**

Reflective statements for your pupils

Why not encourage children to take on some responsibility for singing well? By using these statements they can think about how well they have mastered some of the techniques you have been teaching them.

- I can stand/sit up straight when I sing
- I understand why I warm up before singing
- I can warm up my voice well
- I can sing with enthusiasm
- I can sing the song accurately
- I can sing without shouting
- I can sing loudly and softly
- I can sing the lyrics clearly
- I can communicate the meaning of the lyrics
- I can listen at the same time as singing
- I can make my voice blend well with the group

Dress rehearsal

Practise running the song as a dress rehearsal in the space where the performance will take place. Different acoustics in different rooms can make a big difference to how it feels to sing even a very familiar song. In a bigger space than the choir is used to, they will need to be reminded to sing to the person standing at the back of the hall – not necessarily louder, you don't want them straining their voices, but projecting. Just looking at the back of the hall when they sing will help them do this.

Finally, remind them to smile when they sing. It transforms the sound and is much more engaging for the audience.

Tip ▷ **Join a choir**

> If you are not confident about conducting, join a choir yourself and watch what the conductor does. You can learn a huge amount from being on the opposite side.

Top ten tips for leading your choir

Despite all the variations and possibilities, there are some things which all choirs have in common. Here are our top ten tips on leading your school choir:

Choose songs children and staff will enjoy and sing well. What warm-ups and songs will you use over the coming weeks? Do you have a balance of songs, e.g. some that are quick to pick up, something with a bit more learning involved, a classic that everyone will enjoy for instance? Are the songs appropriate for the age of your singers? Think about the range, how difficult the tune is and how complicated the words and rhythms are.

❶ INCLUDE EVERYONE

Singing is great fun and has the power to bring people together. Think about how to make at least one of your choirs fully inclusive and accessible to all pupils in your school.

❷ PLAN AND GET PREPPED

Have a sense of what you want to achieve and set some achievable goals, e.g. regular rehearsals, a termly performance, to gain confidence in your leading, to improve singing quality.

❸ PICK YOUR WARM-UPS AND SONGS

Start with simple, unison pieces aiming to sing them really well and gradually build the level of challenge and skill development. Consider the suitability of songs for the age of your singers, e.g. lyrics, musical complexity, how low and high the song goes. A healthy 'diet' of singing should be rich and diverse, so cover a broad range of styles, including pop, classical, world music, traditional, *a cappella* and accompanied. Keep in mind your pupils' opinions and preferences too, and consider them when making your choices.

❹ BE CONFIDENT IN YOUR ABILITY TO LEAD

If you need some encouragement, reread Chapter 4 and brush up on your Singing Leader Checklist.

❺ GET OTHERS INVOLVED

Get other teachers, staff, parents or older pupils involved. Anyone who loves music, is enthusiastic or who can play piano or guitar would be a great asset. Older students might want to gain some experience of leading, so think about opportunities that will help them develop their skills. Reread the section on Young Singing Leaders in Chapter 4.

6 LISTEN TO YOUR SINGERS

Give them constructive feedback discussing ways to improve as well as telling them what's working. Use recordings of the songs you are learning to demonstrate and familiarise pupils with them. Get them to practise their listening skills – set them listening tasks so they learn how to listen in a focussed way. Listening is a core musicianship skill that they will need to develop over time.

7 KEEP VOCAL HEALTH IN MIND

Look after the singers' voices, and your own. Refresh your knowledge by rereading Chapter 3.

Golden rules are:

1. Warm up and cool down each time you lead a singing session.
2. Don't over-sing. Don't sing for too long without breaks, and don't strain the voice by trying to sing too loudly or outside of a comfortable vocal range.
3. Keep hydrated. Have regular sips of water.
4. Establish and maintain good posture.
5. Relax and support your breath from your stomach.

8 SEIZE OPPORTUNITIES TO PERFORM

Whether to staff, family, friends, pupils, governors, the local community and other schools, it's a chance to be heard, refine your singing and increase confidence. It's also a great way of celebrating your choir's journey and achievements.

9 AS WELL AS SINGING IN UNISON, TRY BRINGING IN SOME HARMONY

Start with rounds, as these prepare pupils for singing in parts. Next attempt some simple part songs.

10 DON'T BE AFRAID TO MAKE IT PLAYFUL AND HAVE SOME FUN!

Include silly songs, games and warm-ups as these will keep students engaged and maintain energy levels.

Choir planner

This space is to help you reflect on what you have read so far, and think about what plans you want to make for your school choirs.

Choir name

Emblem

Min number

Max number

Rehearsal space

Type

Internal events

Date

Open to

1

Rehearsal day

2

Time

3

Rehearsal frequency

4

Other staff involved

External events

Date

1

2

3

Goals

Achieved by

1

2

3

Possible barriers

Solutions

Warm-ups

List below your 'go-to' warm-ups and songs that you will try first because you
think they will work with your singers and which you feel most confident about leading.

First warm-ups	First songs
1 Physical	1
2 Vocal	2
3 Vocal	3
4 Vocal	4

How will you explain why warm-ups are important?

1

2

3

Do you have any Young Singing Leaders in mind? Which warm-ups might you get them to try?

👤	Warm-up
👤	

Sing with good posture

Is everyone sitting or standing tall?	
Are shoulders loose?	
Are neck and spine aligned?	
Are heads facing forwards?	

Command attention

Can all your singers see you?	
Can they all hear you?	
Have you got eye contact from everyone?	

What are your tried-and-tested ways of gaining your singers' attention? Check-in with yourself regularly that you are not resorting to shouting – you don't want to lose your voice.

1
2
3

Repertoire

Which are your personal absolute favourite songs? What do you love about them?
Do you have an arrangement of them which will suit your choir?

1 Title	Artist/Composer
2	
3	

Your choir's first repertoire

1 Title	Artist/Composer
2	
3	
4	
5	

Song 1

👤 Singing Leader

No. of teaching weeks		Do they know it already?	Y	N
Start week		Do you need sheetmusic?	Y	N
Finish week		Accompaniment?	Y	N

Teaching ideas

Accomp. type

Song 2

👤 Singing Leader

No. of teaching weeks		Do they know it already?	Y	N
Start week		Do you need sheetmusic?	Y	N
Finish week		Accompaniment?	Y	N

Teaching ideas

Accomp. type

Song 3

👤 Singing Leader

No. of teaching weeks		Do they know it already?	Y	N
Start week		Do you need sheetmusic?	Y	N
Finish week		Accompaniment?	Y	N

Teaching ideas

Accomp. type

Song 4

👤 Singing Leader

No. of teaching weeks		Do they know it already?	Y	N
Start week		Do you need sheetmusic?	Y	N
Finish week		Accompaniment?	Y	N

Teaching ideas

Accomp. type

9

MAKING PROGRESS AND IMPROVING SINGING

While much of what we have been thinking about so far has been about extending the range of contexts for singing in school and achieving inclusion in singing activity for every child, you will also want to be working towards improving the quality of the singing that is taking place.

We know that the quality of children's singing is better when the quality of the vocal leadership is good. We also know that an understanding of the principles of good vocal health and technique will support good singing. These are covered in Chapters 3 and 4. In this chapter, we are going to think about ways to improve the quality of the singing you are hearing when you are in your school; how to recognise good singing; how to spot areas that would benefit from support, guidance and practice; and, suggestions and techniques for helping your young singers to make those improvements and adjustments over time.

It needs to be recognised first that every school will be working from their own starting point, as will each individual child and so 'improvement' will mean a range of different things in different contexts and stages. In our view, this isn't about benchmarking particular vocal targets that ought to be achieved by a given age. It isn't helpful to create a set of age-based goals that don't take account of the different backgrounds children come from, their varying stages of musical and physical development, and other developmental factors which will affect what they can reasonably be expected to achieve. These factors may include:

■ Whether the child has a musical culture in the home, where music has been part of home-life from birth
■ Whether the child has already had the opportunity to learn an instrument or sing in school or other settings
■ The physical development of the child
■ Whether the child has any special needs or disabilities
■ Whether the school itself already has some culture of singing, or none.

Improving the quality of singing in your school requires three things:
1. A conscious commitment from you and other staff to improve the quality of singing.
2. Your ability to hear and to identify what can be improved, and, over time, the children's ability to do the same.
3. Knowledge of some techniques and approaches to allow you to support the singers to make those improvements with practice.

It can be taken bit by bit and is a commitment over time, so don't be disheartened if you feel there is a way to go. We will help you to make a plan in this chapter so you know how to tackle common aspects of singing for young voices which need support and guidance for improvements to be made.

Conditions for improvement

There are some overall conditions you can foster within your school which will go a long way to helping the quality of singing to improve organically over time.

Role models and inspiration

Having good singing role models among the staff and older pupils will be inspiring for your younger singers. Opportunities to hear and see others singing well and enjoying their singing will set a great example. If you can establish a staff choir for example, that would be really great for the pupils to see and hear, and they will be really encouraging and proud of their teachers for getting up and singing to them in an assembly every once in a while, instead of the other way around.

Visiting guest singers, vocal leaders and choirs will also be a source of inspiration and can motivate pupils and teachers to want to sing well. It is also a chance to learn about other styles of singing and musical genres and to hear more advanced singers sing live – always a powerful experience.

Take them out of school to gain a range of singing experiences, either where they get to sing, or they get to hear others sing, or both. This raises aspirations and helps pupils see what they might be able to achieve.

Make connections, think about progression routes

Make connections with other schools, do joint singing events, maybe work with your local secondary school and have some older students come and visit and perform or lead some singing themselves. While making these external connections you can be thinking about potential progression routes for some of your young singers who would benefit from a new challenge – might they be able to join a local choir outside of school which is at a more advanced level? Could they take part in a Big Sing event run by a local organisation? Are any of them showing a particular leaning towards musical theatre and would potentially benefit from joining a local theatre school after school or at weekends? Could the theatre school or another local organisation come into school and run a workshop or series of workshops with the children? Could they provide training or professional development for you or other members of school staff?

You can be thinking as well about the progression routes for young singers within your own school from nursery through to joining the choir or becoming a young singing leader.

Sing regularly and practise

Where are the opportunities for your pupils to sing regularly? Is there an appropriate space in which you can practise and rehearse? Are there regular opportunities for the pupils to perform songs they have learnt? These don't need to be formal concerts every time, it could be as simple as performing to another class or to the head teacher one afternoon. All these give a focus for improving and perfecting a song ready to sing to someone else.

Start from where you are

In order to understand where you are starting from you are going to need to use your ears to really listen to the singing that is taking place in your school. Whether you would consider yourself to be 'musical' or not, most humans have a strong sense of when music sounds good and when it doesn't. What you may need to fine-tune is your ability to pinpoint and analyse what is good, what is not so good, why it sounds right or doesn't sound right, before you can begin to make a strategy for improvement.

Listening is the most important skill a musician can possess. It can take a while to learn how to actively listen to music, but the more you listen purposefully to music, the more your ears will tune-in and pass more and more detailed information across to your brain. Even for musicians who are experts at listening to and performing a particular style of music, when hearing an unfamiliar style for the first time it is not immediately understood. Take jazz for example, which can be a very complex form of musical language that may not make sense when we first encounter it. However, through repeated listening, familiarity and some study of what is actually going on in the music, your ear can be trained to tune into this form of musical language so that you then can appreciate the artistry of the performance and the musical language being used can communicate something to you.

Focussed listening

A great starting point is to listen to lots of recordings of choirs – children's or adult choirs – and try these things:

- If you read music, have a copy of the music in front of you when you are listening and follow one line.
- Try and pick out some of the other parts. Do you find it easier to hear the highest or lowest voices? What about the voices in the middle?
- Practise thinking ahead and trying to hear in your head what is coming next, then whether the actual sound matches your imagined sound – in doing this you will be forming expectations in your mind which will either be met or not met by what you hear.
- Now try listening to different choirs' recordings of the same pieces.
- Listen and compare how they differ. They might both be good but try to spot the differences in how the two choirs sing the same piece.

■ Try to describe those differences in words and explain what you prefer from the two performances and why.

Or, even better, go to a concert where a choir is singing:

■ While you are listening think about what you like about the singing.
■ What kind of sound do they make?
■ How might you put the sound into words to describe it to someone else?
■ Notice the phrasing, the dynamics, how together they are, how they enunciate the words. Again, try to think about how you would describe what is good about it in words.

Best of all, join a choir! You will learn so much from the experience of singing with others yourself, learning to listen to the voices around you, to blend your voice with theirs and working collectively on a blended sound and polished performance.

What you are learning here is the ability to listen deeply to a performance and identify what you like about it. The next stage is to learn how to articulate that in words – the better you get at this the more able you will be to describe to your choir or singing group what it is that you want to hear in their singing.

Tip 〉〉	**Like teacher, like pupil**

Listening to recordings, attending concerts, learning to listen deeply and identify what they like about the singing and being able to explain it in words – all these are things your pupils can do too, and it will help them develop as singers and musicians.

Focussed listening in the classroom

Whatever the context of singing in your school, whether in the classroom, in assembly, in music lessons or in choir, you want your pupils to be singing well and to be improving. So, keeping in mind the golden rule of starting where they are, if you apply some listening and improving techniques in any of those contexts, you will be able to help the children to learn, enjoy and improve the quality of their singing.

The focussed listening technique isn't something you need to keep to yourself and take sole responsibility for. Constantly encourage your pupils to be listening to themselves and each other – to the sound of the group – when they are singing, and to be asking themselves questions about whether it could be improved.

Here is a list of the kind of things that you, and they, can be listening out for, broken down into categories:

Pulse and rhythm

- Are we keeping a steady pulse, or are we rushing, or slowing down compared with the pulse at the start?
- How does the pulse feel? Does it feel about right for the music?
- Does it feel like the music is dragging, or too sluggish?
- Does it feel like the music is too rushed or frantic?
- Do the words feel garbled?
- Does the pulse feel appropriate for the mood of the song and the meaning of the words? You could make them laugh about this by telling them to imagine a funeral march played really quickly or a happy up-beat song played really, really slowly, for example, music used to accompany the clowns in a circus. Have them think about and describe why this wouldn't feel right.
- Have we got the rhythms accurate? Are we singing them together or are they sounding messy?

Pitch and melodic accuracy

- How well have we learnt the music? Are there mistakes we can hear?
- Are we listening to each other carefully to make sure our intonation is good?
- Are we listening carefully to the accompaniment or backing track (if there is one) to make sure we are in tune?
- Are we able to sing the correct notes cleanly?
- Are we swooping when there are jumps in pitch or able to manage the jumps cleanly?
- When singing in parts – can we hear the other parts? Are we listening carefully to them to make sure we are in tune with each other?

Tone, blend and balance

- Are we producing a nice blended sound together?
- Are any voices sticking out?
- Is the sound we are making going to be pleasant to listen to?
- Is it a nice focussed sound – not breathy or shouty?
- When singing in parts, are the parts balanced? Can we hear the other parts as well as our own?

Communication and expression

- Are we singing the words clearly?
- Does the way we are singing the song help to communicate its meaning?
- Are we singing with a sense of the style of the music?
- Are we singing loudly and softly in the right places?
- Are our faces expressing the mood of the song?

These are just examples and the children won't be able to do all of these things to begin with but they are good indicators of the kinds of things you, and they, can be listening for when they are singing.

Improving what you hear

What can we do when we (and they) spot that something isn't quite right? First of all, as educators we know that the following approaches to rehearsal and practice won't be effective:

- Asking the children to repeat something over and over without pointing out what they should be improving.
- Always starting at the beginning and singing through the whole thing without focussed practice on the less well-known or tricky bits.
- Not connecting their learning, for example, not connecting the warm-up with something specific they need to practise and transferring that learning into the song.

> **Tip** **Break it down, slow it down**
>
> 1. Identify the section or sections that are causing problems and practise just those sections slowly but in time, i.e. the section is still in time with itself and rhythmically accurate, it is just slower than the actual tempo you are aiming for.
>
> 2. Break the troublesome sections down into really short phrases, practise them slowly.
>
> 3. When the short phrases are accurate, try putting them back together, still below tempo.
>
> 4. Gradually increase the tempo, making sure that there is still accuracy.

We also need to remember, whenever we are teaching, that children have different strengths and preferences in their learning styles. So, we need to use multiple approaches to solving each problem – some young singers will feel how to improve, some will hear how to improve and others will need to understand intellectually how to improve. Mostly, you need a mix of all three.

Here are some specific things you can try in order to make improvements under the four headings we used above: Pulse and rhythm; Pitch and melodic accuracy; Tone, blend and balance; Communication and expression.

Pulse and rhythm

Much of acquiring and improving a good sense of pulse and rhythm is about internalising it, within the body and mind. The best way to achieve this is with a holistic approach – covering feeling, hearing and thinking.

Feeling

Some children will respond most positively to actualising the pulse and rhythm within their bodies. Stepping in time with the pulse, clapping the off-beat, inventing and using body percussion – all these can help with achieving this. This approach isn't only applicable to music with a strong drum-beat (like rock and pop), it applies just as much to classical, folk and other genres of music. This internalising of the pulse is a thread that runs through all musical performance on any instrument.

Hearing

Some children will also benefit from listening and matching a pulse. Drummers spend hours and hours practising with a metronome or click-track for a reason. It's also the reason why the drummer at football matches is vital to keep everyone in the stadium together. So try creating a steady, audible beat for the children to sing to – not the accompaniment, and not the backing track, just an audible beat on its own. This might be as simple as you clapping the beat if you are confident you can keep it really steady, or you can use a metronome. You can buy a regular metronome in music shops or you can use a free online metronome that you can run through speakers.

> **Tip** ⟩ **Keeping in time**
>
> There are free metronome apps you can download onto your phone or tablet. Some of these have a feature that enables you to tap a pulse into the app and have it give you the metronome marking of that pulse. Very useful!

Thinking

Finally, an intellectual understanding of what is going on rhythmically is also important and helpful. This is where a bit of understanding of music theory and notation will really help. A major part of rhythmic accuracy comes from the ability to sub-divide the beat (breaking it down into smaller component parts) silently in your mind (your musical computer) or physically in your body.

Explaining to your pupils that one of these notes ♪ is worth half of one of these notes ♩ and then getting them to feel or clap two quavers evenly and steadily within one crotchet beat, will cement and enhance their intellectual understanding of what is going on in the music. It will also dramatically improve the accuracy of their note placement.

Troubleshooting: Pulse and rhythm

How do I know if we are maintaining a steady pulse or rushing or slowing down?

If you are singing to a backing track, you will spot that something is adrift pretty quickly because, unlike a kindly pianist, it won't slow down or speed up in sympathy with you. If you are singing *a cappella*, the ability to keep the same pulse throughout is entirely on the singers and your guidance of them, and will require strong internalisation of the beat – physically and mentally.

How do I know the speed of the track?

The metronome mark will often be given at the top of the first stave of the sheet music and will look something like this: $\quarternote = 100$. This one tells you that if you set a metronome to 100BPM, you will get the crotchet beat of the song. If the song is in the time signature 4/4, there are 4 crotchet beats in each bar.

If you don't have the sheet music or the metronome marking isn't given, you will have to work it out by trial and error on your metronome. Practise the song while listening carefully to a metronome beat. Once you think you have got it, test it out by singing a section without the metronome then test that you are still in time by starting up the metronome again.

> **Tip** » **BPM**
>
> A metronome marking of 60 means there are 60 beats per minute – in other words, one beat per second. So even without a metronome you can use this to make an approximation of the tempo.

The rhythms are sounding messy and we are not together, how do I make them more accurate?

Identify which rhythmic patterns in the song are proving difficult. Is it a recurring rhythmic pattern? If you solve it in one place, will that help with several tricky corners in the song?

Are the lyrics adding to the complexity? You could try singing it to 'la' 'ba' or 'da,' whichever feels right for the context. A 'da' or 'ba' will give you clearer articulation of each note than 'la' will, so 'la' might be better for a flowing melodic line but 'da' or 'ba' might be better for something more percussive.

Conversely, you can practise separating the tune from the words and practise speaking the words to the rhythm, or you could try practising clapping the rhythm before trying to sing it.

Getting your singers to sub-divide longer notes for greater precision and accuracy will also help, coupled with developing their intellectual understanding of the relationship between the different note values. Treat it as a maths problem, underpinned by physically feeling the sub-division of the beats. Do this with clapping – you could split the group in two and have one group clapping on-beats and the other clapping off-beats – or try using the thinking voice.

Pitch and melodic accuracy

All singers, from beginners to professionals, sometimes have problems with pitch. Don't let anyone tell you otherwise. Make it clear to your students that there is always another level to aspire to and that you are going to try some fun activities with them that are aimed at improving their tuning.

Humming

Blending with other singers helps individuals to come into pitch. Hum a mid-range note – G or A – and walk around the class, passing the hum to each child. Tell the children to breathe when they need to. The action of passing it is very important. Put your own hands to your mouth and lift the hum out. Pass it to the pupil's hands, humming all the time. They must then put the hum into their own mouths. The actions help to concentrate the child's listening powers. You will be amazed at the result. When all the children are humming, encourage them to open up to an 'ah'.

Concentration

Good tuning requires intense concentration. During some call-and-response exercises ask them to lightly cup (not clamp) their hands over their ears, as if they were a pair of large headphones. Point out how you can hear your own voice more clearly. Work on a few middle-range notes and see how this helps to improve tuning. Make it clear that this is only an exercise and is not to be used while they are singing a song.

Simple harmony

Simple harmony singing can also help to improve tuning. Just take a major third – F and A. Ask all the children to sing the notes one after the other and then divide the class down the middle. One half sings the F, the other the A. Encourage them to hold their note while being aware of the other. As they try to preserve the major third they will bring their own note more into tune.

Reaching the higher notes

It is often a struggle for children to sing higher notes comfortably. It is best not to take too much direct action on increasing range with young children. Vocal health must be our prime consideration. But there are some fun exercises that will gently encourage them to be aware of their higher voices.

- **Diving board**: Imagine you are on the top board at the swimming pool. Stretch your arm and finger as high as you can to indicate this. Find the highest gentle note in your voice, and dive off the board, sliding the voice down as you approach the water, using your full range. Add a deep 'splash!' at the end. Imagine you have videoed this. Reverse the film, starting from the 'splash!' and ending up back on the board.
- **Yoo hoo!**: You have just spotted your best friend over the other side of the road. All together now... "Yoo hoo!" Point out that the top "Yoo" can be turned into a fully sounded high-note. Show them, if possible.
- **Diaphragm support**: All singing requires breath support, but if you can point out the particular link between diaphragm support and higher notes then you will plant some good seeds. Get them to place their hands on the lower part of their rib cage, with some of the hand below the bottom rib. Then do a stage laugh, Father Christmas is a good example to mimic. Sing "Yo ho ho" and ask them to tell you what is happening to your hands. Take some higher notes and "Yo ho ho" on those, getting them to

see the link with your breathing. Then drop the consonants and sing "ah ah ah". Ask them to join in. Don't try to sustain the notes at this stage, just touch them briefly.

Troubleshooting: Pitch and melodic accuracy

How do I stop us from singing flat?

This might be a combination of singing consistently 'under the note', under-hitting particular intervals or jumps, or going flat when singing descending scales.

If there is a tendency for your singers to sing consistently under the note, posture, technical remedies and reminding them to listen to each other are usually the first places to start. As before, combining feeling, hearing and thinking together will be really effective.

- **Feeling**: Try refreshing posture and technique by standing, doing some warm-up exercises and to focus their vocal tone (use the exercise for breathiness below).
- **Hearing**: Combine this with asking them to listen carefully to each other and to the accompaniment (if there is one).
- **Thinking**: Think about singing on the tops of the notes rather than reaching up towards them.

If there are particular problems with jumps that they are under-hitting you can try the following:

- **Feeling**: Practising swooping up to the note will help your singers learn and remember where in their voices the note is, how big the gap between the two notes is, and what it feels like in their voice.
- **Hearing**: Sing the bottom note of the problem interval out loud, pause, hear the upper note in your thinking voice, then sing it. Practise this a few times for accuracy.
- **Thinking**: Thinking about the distance between the two notes; thinking about singing on the top of that note; thinking about coming down and landing on the top of it, rather than reaching up to it.

And problems with descending scales going flat can be helped by simply thinking 'up' while singing it. Try getting your singers to do a smooth upwards movement with outstretched hands, palms facing upwards while they are singing the descending scale. You will be surprised how much that can trick the brain into thinking upwards while singing downwards.

How do I stop us from singing sharp?

It is much more common for singers to sing consistently flat than sharp, but when inexperienced singers are excited or nervous, e.g. in a performance, they can suddenly begin singing sharp even if they never have before. Good listening skills are your best ally here. Encouraging them to listen carefully to each other, the accompaniment and to their own voices and making performance a regular occurrence – even if it is on a small scale to another class or just another teacher – will all help to avoid sudden onsets of sharp singing.

The other thing to watch out for is that your pupils are not singing sharp because the song is too low for them. So if the sharp singing is coupled with poor tone or signs of voices giving out on the low notes, consider transposing it up a tone.

My KS2 choir is struggling to maintain their tuning throughout a song.

Tonality refers to the key you are in or the 'home' note of a particular song (the tonic). Developing a sense of this 'home-ness' and being really grounded in the feeling of being in a key can help your singers remain in tune, especially if they are singing *a cappella* and have no accompaniment to latch onto.

Sing a scale up and down to: "1,2,3,4,5,6,7,8, 8,7,6,5,4,3,2,1". Sing once more, this time only going up to 5 and back down. Try singing again but this time put 2 and 4 into your thinking voice. You should now hear notes 1, 3 and 5 out loud. Divide the group into three each taking one of the notes: 1, 3 and 5. This is a major triad. Sing them to 'mm', 'ng' or a vowel sound. In the scale of C, you will sing: C, E and G. Sing them simultaneously and listen carefully to each other. Then swap notes so they are singing a different note of the triad, repeat until they have sung all 3 notes, and have listened to those notes in their voices and the resonance of the triad.

Now starting on number 5, G, sing up five notes from there and then find the triad. These notes will be: G, B and D. Practise as you did before with everyone getting a turn at singing all three notes and listening carefully to the whole sound. If this is high for singers do a quick siren or only have the highest voices on the top note.

Finally, you are going to hold up one finger when you want them to sing the first triad (C, E & G) and five fingers when you want them to sing the second triad (G, B and D). Get them to practise moving smoothly from one to the other and hear how each time they return to one, it is like returning to the home triad. Tell them that these are two chords that often end a piece.

Next, you are going to ask them to hold the home triad (C, E and G) in their minds while singing any other notes they want – anything other than the notes they are on – the more random the cacophony of sound at this point the better. Then on your signal they are going to return home to C, E and G, by reverting to the memory of the sound plus listening to each other and gradually arriving in the right place.

Before you sing a song where you know they will struggle to hold onto the tonality and remain in the right key, do this exercise in the key of the song in question and try to get them to really absorb and memorise what being in that key feels and sounds like. It's also a great way of getting them to really open their ears and listen to each other within the overall sound.

Tip 〉〉 **Repertoire idea**

The song *Nanuma* in the Sing Up Song bank is a lovely round for practising tuning in a major key.

Tone, blend and balance

Achieving a good tone, blend and balance is almost entirely about developing good listening skills and good vocal technique. If the tone the singers are producing doesn't sound good, it is most likely that there's something you can do to remedy that in relation to their posture, how they are breathing and by making sure the song is within the correct range for their voices. Warm-ups are a great way to address tone problems (see Warm-up 5, page 30).

Breathiness

Remind them to focus the sound so it isn't breathy. Experiment with getting them to all hum to a focussed and unforced 'mm' or 'ng' sound. Try it on one note or on a triad if you are singing in parts, and encourage them to really listen to the resonance of their voices. Next, still using the 'mm' or 'ng' sounds, sing through the song. Repeat the song with the same tone, but open up to an 'oo' sound, then an 'oh', and finally an 'ah', but not with an overly opened mouth, just a natural 'ah' sound. Last of all, add the words, asking them to consciously try to retain the same sound they have just been making (also, see Warm-up 4, page 29).

Shouting

Don't let exuberance and enthusiasm turn into shouty singing. Take the whole dynamic range of the song down a notch if necessary so there is room for a noticeable increase in volume for the loud bits without resorting to over-singing them.

Just keeping conscious of not shouting in your mind and in the children's minds will probably be sufficient to avoid it happening. Your gestures from the front will serve as an effective limiter on the volume they are aiming for, so when you can hear it going too far, think about what gestures you can use to rein it in without losing the excitement of the louder moments.

Basic, practical things like the singers straining to be heard over a backing track or piano accompaniment that is too loud can be swiftly dealt with and may solve the problem.

Ensemble singing

Achieving good blend and balance is about sounding as one – an ensemble. Just like in a sports team, each player is valued and essential as an individual but ultimately they must all work together as a team to be successful. In singing this will mean:

- Listening to and watching each other
- Beginning and ending phrases together
- Placing words carefully at the same time with the same clear articulation
- Singing precisely the same rhythms
- Singing with the same phrasing and breathing
- Being aware of the overall volume
- Having a shared sense of style and meaning of a song
- Listening to the overall sound and consciously blending their own voice with it.

Creating a unison blend

Achieving a good blend among your singers requires a combination of a consistent, shared tone quality, uniformity of pronunciation – including uniformity of vowel sounds and precise placing of consonants – and phrasing the music as one. You are looking for a collective unison sound, not a group of individual singers. The responsibility for this lies with your singers themselves but you can guide them as to how to achieve this and encourage them to listen carefully to each other. If you tell them that you don't want to hear individual voices sticking out and encourage them to listen to each other and to try to blend their sound with their neighbour, this will really help them to become much more conscious of how they are contributing to an overall sound rather than just how they are singing as individuals.

It can help if you listen to smaller groups or rows of singers and move them around to encourage them to listen to each other more carefully. They will focus their listening on the things you are listening for. Discussing where you want them to breathe and how you want them to pronounce words and vowel sounds in particular will help with consistency. You will also want them to have a shared understanding of the style of the song and how you want that conveyed in their singing. For example, a lullaby will require a different style of singing to a sea shanty. It's worth discussing this and getting them to think about and describe what the differences are.

Encourage them to watch you when they are singing and be super-clear with your gestures about when and how you want them to sing. You can help them to begin and end each phrase at the same time and breathe in the correct place between phrases.

Moving into part-singing – developing balance

When you are ready to move into part-singing, you will need to begin thinking about achieving a good balance between different parts. This doesn't necessarily mean that all parts should be heard equally. Generally speaking, you will want to hear the melody more prominently than the other parts but overall it is about achieving an appropriate balance for the music. There will be times when the melody is in the top part and other times when it is in one of the lower parts and you will need to tell your singers to be listening out for it and adjusting their own singing to ensure that the melody can always be heard. At other times you might want to bring out a particular phrase in one of the other parts – perhaps a phrase that lends musical interest or colour to the music at that point. You can direct this visually and make your singers aware of what you are wanting them to be listening for and thinking about what the audience can hear too.

Communication and expression

Music is a performance art and as such its main purpose is to communicate meaning to an audience. The voice is the most naturally expressive instrument and the only one that can actually employ words to aid in communication. So it is particularly important that as singers we pay attention to how we are communicating the meaning of the words and the music when we sing. It is also important to remember that we have our whole bodies with which to communicate that meaning, not just our voices. Our facial expressions and how we stand and move (even if only subtly) all contribute to how we communicate meaning through our performance and when this is done as a group in a choir, it is all the more powerful and expressive.

The first and most simple point is to tell the singers to make sure that the words can be heard by the audience. The work you have already done on achieving consistent vowel sounds, clear articulation of consonants and phrasing will help with this. But you should also make sure that the singers understand and are thinking about the meaning of the words when they are singing and that they are consciously using their voices and facial expressions to communicate that meaning. Ask them to think about some of their favourite singers and actors and what they observe about the way they communicate meaning through their delivery of spoken lines or sung phrases, and how their facial expressions help them to do that.

It can be amusing to have them sing songs in completely the wrong style to emphasise how to get it wrong, for example, singing a lullaby aggressively, singing 'Happy Birthday' like a mournful dirge. You can make the point that the notes are the same but their interpretation is dramatically changing the emotion and meaning.

Line and phrasing

- Have some fun speaking a sentence in a steady, dry monotone and immediately contrast it with a lively, normal delivery. Try: 'I went to the Ed Sheeran concert on Saturday and it was the most fantastic night of my life.' Or: 'In the last minute of the game Jamie Vardy shot through the centre, dodged two defenders, and scored. It was unbelievable!' Discuss with the children where the important words are. How would the speaker be feeling? How does the listener know they are feeling that?
- Take a song they know and decide with the children where breaths can be taken. Let them see how these decisions are made – breath capacity, the sense of the words, the rhythm of the line. Discuss where the focal point of the line is and work towards it and away from it. Use the breath

to carry you through the consonants so that you get a good legato (smooth line).
- Use movement and gesture whenever you can to get across the idea of musical shape.
- Use Warm-up 6: Clarifying articulation, page 30.

Dynamics

- Involving your pupils with decision-making about dynamics within a song will engage them in the thought process of what these will bring to the meaning and performance. There may already be dynamic markings in the music which you will follow, but you will want to discuss these, talk about why the composer or arranger has put them there and ask your pupils what they think the intention was behind those markings.
- If you are creating your own dynamics, start with the meaning of the words and ask your pupils what dynamics they think would help to communicate that meaning expressively. Ask them to articulate why they are making that suggestion, and even better to demonstrate it.
- To practise crescendo (getting louder) and diminuendo (getting quieter), ask them to sing any vowel sound on a single note and indicate louder and quieter with your hands in front of your diaphragm, as if you were playing an accordion. Hands wider – crescendo; hands closer – diminuendo.

Watch out for unwanted pitch changes; insist on careful listening. Remember the caveat about loud singing vs shouting. Neither do you want quiet singing to become breathy. Some practise of singing quietly but with a focussed tone would be helpful.

Expressive faces

- Ask the children to think about the meaning of the words and how they want the audience to feel when hearing the words sung to the music.
- Ask them to speak the words as though they were saying them in real life to someone. What would their facial expressions be in that context?
- A gentle smile covers a multitude of possible moods and will also help the vocal tone be bright and focussed!

TRY THIS

Miming with your hands, screw your face up like a piece of paper, then pull it out as flat as you can.

Over a count of 10, morph from one expression to another. Start with sad and, over 10, gradually transform to radiantly happy. Go from bored to angry or innocent to sly.

Ask a pupil to do one and get the others to guess what the expressions are.

Of course, we shouldn't use our faces in such a contrived way when we sing, but these activities will exercise the facial muscles and remind the children that an expressive face can help so much in the interpretation of songs.

Breath

Some work on breath control can really help with communication and expression in singing – and in making the singing really musical. It is worth remembering though that small bodies have smaller lungs and less refined muscular control, so children won't be able to sing really long phrases in one breath just yet. You can still, however, help them to use their breath to underpin musical and expressive singing.

Like all specialist techniques, it can take years to achieve full mastery of breath control, but much can be achieved with children in the early stages by establishing some basic good practice.

A quick health warning: it's not a good idea to practise extended breathing exercises with young and inexperienced singers. They can get dizzy, and asthma sufferers can experience difficulty. Of course, singing can be very good for those with asthma, but please be cautious when working directly on breathing.

Remind your pupils that when you sing, the whole body is your instrument. Place the feet at hip width and keep the knees loose, making sure that backs are comfortably straight. Try some gentle non-vocal warm-up exercises, paying particular attention to the shoulders. Lift them up to your ears and then drop. They will fall naturally into the correct position.

Children like to know how things work and won't be fobbed off with incomplete answers. Take time to find out how the diaphragm is involved in breathing and practise some simple explanations. Explain that the lungs expand in all directions and that being aware of the movement of the diaphragm helps us breathe more deeply and control the flow of air. Ask the children to place their hands lightly on their 'middles', with the thumb part of the hand on the lower rib cage and the other part below it. Get them to breathe in without raising the shoulders and they will feel some movement under their hands. Make them laugh and point out how their hands are moving with their laughter. If the shoulders are kept relaxed, and not artificially lifted, they will begin to use their diaphragms quite naturally.

As they start to acquire some control over their breathing a whole range of other techniques becomes possible. You will be able to start showing them how singers can spin a mere series of notes and rhythms into something that really communicates – into a living musical performance.

Age group specifics

Singing with 4–7 year olds

■ Songs that inspire actions and movement help children develop their sense of pulse, rhythm and word recall. Start by getting them to step to the pulse and really feel it in their bodies.

■ If you want the children to be focussing their attention on listening to each other and their voices, choose songs with few words and lots of repetition.

■ Young children have much higher voices than adults so it's really important to sing in their range. Go for songs with a tiny range (middle C to A) and have just a few notes that move step-by-step or in small intervals. Bigger jumps are tricky to master for the really young ones.

■ If you can hold a tune, then model singing in your classroom – you don't have to have the greatest voice; just lots of enthusiasm.

Singing with 7–11 year olds

■ As children get older the larynx grows and they can sing an expanding range of notes. A comfortable range is C – C but many will be able to sing higher and/or lower.

■ They will also be gaining more muscular control over their vocal apparatus which will enable them to tackle more intricate melodies and bigger jumps. Their developing aural skills will also help them to navigate these with accuracy.

■ Gradually introduce songs with an increasing range. As they get older, the children will be developing more varied vocal ranges – some will naturally develop higher or lower natural ranges than others.

■ So that every child is getting a good vocal work-out and the opportunity to develop the upper and lower registers of their voices, be sure to encourage them to sing across the entire voice. Remember, not everyone has to sing everything – children who can't manage the top or bottom ends of a song's range can be given an alternative part to sing that is more comfortable for their voice.

■ Sing a range of songs both unaccompanied and accompanied; in unison and in parts. Call-and-response, rounds, and partner songs are easier than lots of harmonies.

■ Sing in different styles so the voice has the opportunity to develop a range of techniques and tonal qualities.

■ Teach children to think about the musical sentences (phrases) and how they can use the breath, dynamics, and phrasing to communicate the meaning to an audience.

Singing with teenagers

■ At adolescence, children's voices start to change. Boys' voices deepen, but girls' voices also change at this time, and if you want teenagers to keep singing, find songs they can sing comfortably without embarrassment. (For more on changing voices, see Chapter 3, page 31.)

■ Teaching words and melody separately is a useful technique. Speaking the words in rhythm encourages rhythmic accuracy and good diction; and singing the tune to a 'mm', 'ng' or 'oo' improves tone and melodic accuracy.

■ Try teaching the song following the notation asking pupils to have a go at sight-reading sections of the songs following the rise and fall of the melody. You can support them with pitching by singing with them or using the piano, then as they become more confident readers, gradually take this crutch away.

■ Ask confident singers to lead sectional rehearsals and instrumentalists to accompany the singers.

■ Sing rounds, partner songs, and songs in parts. Start with countermelodies and progressing to full homophonic and contrapuntal textures.

Make a plan

First of all, let's think about the standard of singing currently in your school. You don't need to make all the judgements yourself, you can ask other staff and parents to listen to the singing too and give you their opinions.

Using the same four categories we have already thought about, make some notes below of observations about the singing that can be heard around the school currently.

Pulse and rhythm

- Do pupils move in time to the music when they sing?
- Can the children keep a steady pulse when singing?
- Do they speed up or slow down?
- How well do they manage when singing unaccompanined or with accompaniment?
- How strong is their sense of rhythm across a range of styles of music, for instance, pop, traditional, blues, reggae?
- Are they singing the trickier rhythmic patterns accurately and together or do they sound messy?

1.

2.

3.

4.

5.

Pitch and melodic accuracy

- How well do pupils listen when you teach a song by rote?
- Do you always sing along with your pupils or can they sing independently of you?
- Can pupils sing music which reaches into their higher and lower voices?
- Are they swooping to notes or managing melodic jumps cleanly?
- Can they sing in tune and with accuracy with and without accompaniment?
- Can they sing well in unison, rounds and parts?

1.

2.

3.

4.

5.

Tone, blend and balance

■ Are pupils in the habit of listening to each other when they are singing?

■ How well can pupils blend their voices to sound like one?

■ Can they adjust the volume of their singing and are they aware of how loud or quiet they are singing?

■ Are they making a nice, natural, focussed sound – not breathy or shouty?

1.

2.

3.

4.

5.

Communication and expression

■ Can you hear the words clearly when the children sing?

■ Do they sing with a sense of the meaning of the words?

■ Can pupils sing expressively across a range of moods and styles?

■ Are the children animated when they sing?

1.

2.

3.

4.

5.

10

YOUR SINGING SCHOOL JOURNEY: SILVER AND GOLD

In this section of the book we look at how to put everything into practice to work towards the Singing School levels Silver, Gold and Platinum.

We will set out some reflective questions and writing space for you to plan your own Singing School journey. Working through these pages should help you to develop a clear strategy that is bespoke to your school and to set some clear goals. From there you can use that thinking and work to build an implementation plan.

Achieving Silver level

So now we're going to get into the detail of how you might go about planning and achieving Silver Level in your school. We've put together some examples of what you might do to meet the criteria. These are only suggestions, some of which might work well in your school context, others might be a creative springboard for you to come up with your own which are more tailored to your pupils and school setting.

As with the criteria, the questions are divided into questions relating to pupils, staff, the senior leadership team and governors and the whole school community. Tick off the ideas that already happen and the ideas that you want to try, and then write down any other ideas applicable to your school that you thought of, or that you have found in this book.

Pupils' singing activity:

Do all pupils sing more than twice a week, in and out of the music lesson?

Singing in your class music lessons is great, and a natural part of how you're probably already teaching music. But for your school to fully benefit from the power of singing, you also need to be singing in other contexts outside of the music lesson.

At Sing Up, we talk about 'smuggling singing into school' because we've found that teachers often have an idea that 'singing' means pupils should be singing complex songs to a very high standard with a choir and worry that they lack the time and skills to achieve that. In fact, we encourage schools to start with just a little singing of very simple songs sprinkled across the school day – of course it would be marvellous to also have a wonderful school choir, but you don't have to start off aiming for that. Better to start with small, manageable steps that every teacher feels they can take on board. Remember to make it clear that a regular sprinkling of singing in class will actually help teachers do their jobs better – not be a time-consuming distraction from the 'real' learning work.

	In progress	Completed
Sing in assembly at least once a week.	☐	☐
Give each class a Sing Up wall chart and encourage them to fill it in weekly.	☐	☐
Learn to read and write routine songs.	☐	☐
Start a playground singing games initiative.	☐	☐

Other ideas

Are pupils given the opportunity to share their singing with their peers?

Finding opportunities for pupils to sing to each other will motivate them to learn songs well and give them a sense of pride in their collective achievement. It also requires teamwork so that no-one lets the rest of the team down. These don't need to be formal 'concerts', just opportunities to sing for other pupils.

	In progress	Completed
Share a class song in an assembly or with a whole Key Stage or year group.	☐	☐
During a themed week, like a STEM or Arts Week, ask the children to bring in a song that they want to share with their peers.	☐	☐
Bring classes that are studying the same topics together and sing as a larger group about the subject.	☐	☐

Other ideas

Do pupils identify ways to improve their singing?

Learning to listen and apply constructive criticism to what they hear is a major aspect of how they will learn to improve and become better musicians. It is also a good skill to learn in life – working towards something together, sharing constructive criticism and working as a team to improve. They will learn far more through working out for themselves what needs improving than they will if the teacher tells them. You will need to model the kinds of things they should be listening out for first of course – for example:

- Are we singing together, or did some of us come in a bit early, or a bit late?
- Do we think that the audience will be able to hear the words clearly?
- Are we making a nice sound, or is it getting 'shouty'?
- Did we all breathe in the correct place?
- Did we sing the quiet parts quiet and the louder parts more strongly?
- Did we all remember the correct actions?

	In progress	Completed
Make recordings of the children singing so they can hear/watch them back and discuss them.	☐	☐
Get children in the habit of discussing what they hear and considering how to improve it. Use the reflective statements on page 114 as a guide.	☐	☐
Explore using your voice in playful ways to make children aware of the range of sounds they can make.	☐	☐
Encourage good vocal health and good singing by warming up before singing and standing up while singing.	☐	☐

Other ideas

Do pupils have the opportunity to contribute ideas to broaden singing activity in the school?

Your pupils should naturally take pride in their singing and want to be actively engaged in helping to make suggestions and decisions about where to take it next. If you encourage this with them it will really snowball and being more engaged in the planning and ideas will enthuse and energise them. You will need to take a common-sense approach to collecting ideas and allow the opportunity for you to check the list and make judgements about appropriate suggestions. It might also be an opportunity for some of the children to take leadership roles in the planning or leading of singing at school.

	In progress	Completed
Encourage teachers to ask pupils to suggest songs for the Sing Up wall chart.	☐	☐
Ask children to vote for their favourite songs each week and find out why that song was their favourite.	☐	☐
Ask the children to bring in songs that they'd like to sing and share with their class.	☐	☐

Other ideas

Staff singing activity:

Have all your staff been introduced to singing and encouraged to support the Singing School Coordinator by getting involved?

This is about the school and all the staff making a commitment to becoming a Singing School. In Chapter 2 we talked about the role of the Singing School Coordinator in getting the rest of the staff on board and gave some suggestions about how you might go about doing this. You might want to recap this now.

	In progress	Completed
Hold a singing presentation to tell them about plans to become a Singing School and the benefits of singing.	☐	☐
Reassure staff that informal every-day singing is an important part of being a Singing School – it isn't just about having an amazing choir.	☐	☐
Organise a 'Song of the Week' and get the staff to take it in turns to pick this weekly song.	☐	☐
Introduce all your colleagues to some songs to get them started.	☐	☐
Start a staff choir after school. You could also invite parents and pupils to join.	☐	☐

Other ideas

Do at least two staff regularly lead singing?

For singing to become embedded in your school it needs to be a normalised occurrence for everyone. This means you need as many staff as possible to feel able to lead singing themselves, not just the Singing School Coordinator. So, start small and get at least one other member of staff to a point where they feel confident to lead singing without you, then you can gradually persuade more and more of your colleagues to leave their inhibitions behind and get involved. Your colleagues will need some pointers and guidance to help them to lead singing well – the better they become at it, the more confident and enthusiastic they will feel, and this confidence and enthusiasm is contagious once you get it started.

	In progress	Completed
With a colleague, or two, choose some songs to build up your school's repertoire.	☐	☐
Consider different roles other staff can take in singing sessions, like assemblies.	☐	☐
Encourage non-teaching staff to lead singing, for example, in the playground.	☐	☐
Organise an end of term performance where each class is led by their own teacher.	☐	☐
Encourage colleagues to sing instructions to their class and explain the benefits.	☐	☐

Other ideas

Do staff support the development of vocal work across the school day and support all children's contribution to singing?

For singing to benefit the whole school, every child needs to be involved regularly. Once singing has become 'normalised' in everyday school life, some less confident children may surprise you (and themselves) with how their voices and confidence grow in tandem with one another. Singing is a very inclusive activity so consider also how you can incorporate singing into sessions to support the learning of English for those with English as an additional language. Also for children with special needs or behavioural issues – make sure they are included too. Have another look at Chapter 6 for more information and ideas.

	In progress	Completed
Encourage staff to identify times across the day where they could add singing.	☐	☐
Incorporate singing into EAL (English as an Additional Language) sessions.	☐	☐
Think about ways for all children to be included in singing.	☐	☐

Other ideas

Do staff understand the basics of good vocal health?

Young voices are vulnerable to strain and can be damaged by misuse. Teachers themselves are prone to voice-strain which can be a big problem when you need your voice as a core tool of your job. Obviously, there are more complexities that come into play with more advanced singing technique – some of these are covered in Chapter 3 on Vocal Health. How can you make all your staff aware of the basics of vocal health?

	In progress	Completed
Hold a meeting to introduce the basics of good vocal health to colleagues.	☐	☐
Discuss techniques to save their voices: take breaks, sip water regularly, keep rooms well ventilated, warm-ups.	☐	☐
Provide the staff with warm-ups they can use every day with their classes.	☐	☐

Other ideas

Senior leadership team and governors' involvement

Do the senior leadership team and governors endorse the decision to become a Singing School and are they committed to ensuring that all members of the school know about and support the process? Does singing support the School Development Plan and wider school planning?

To be a Singing School requires a strong commitment from all key stakeholders in school strategy and planning. Singing needs to be written into the school's key strategy documents so that it isn't an after-thought but is a core tool for making school improvement happen. Take a 'head and heart' approach to persuading the team to get behind becoming a Singing School. Some of them will be most persuaded by facts, research evidence and case studies, some will be much more persuaded by seeing and hearing some children singing. So provide both. We've already covered the facts and research evidence in Chapter 1. For the 'heart' part, if you already have some enthusiastic, joyful singing going on in your school that you want to spread more widely, make sure that your leadership team and governors get to hear and see it. Alternatively, find a local school which already has a strong commitment to singing and take a group of the leadership team and governors along to a singing assembly so they can hear the children and also get the opportunity to talk to staff at that school. Peer to peer endorsement is very powerful.

	In progress	Completed
Discuss wth governors the benefits of becoming a Singing School and consider where singing could support wider school aims.	☐	☐
Develop singing-based targets: 'Use singing as a tool to support the development of speech and language learning', or 'Use singing to reinforce and build a strong school community and underpin school ethos'.	☐	☐
Incorporate singing into your school's policy documents: in your SEND policy advocate the use of singing to support social, emotional and behavioural development and speech and language skills.	☐	☐
Suggest that some staff use becoming a Singing School as a performance or CPD goal for the year	☐	☐
Start a staff choir after school. You could also invite parents and pupils to join.	☐	☐
Other ideas		

Whole school community involvement

Does the whole school sing together at least once a week?

Obviously some schools without a very large space will find this difficult. It is about bringing together as large a group as practically possible for some regular shared singing. This could be in an assembly, across a Key Stage or year group. Whatever is most appropriate for you.

	In progress	Completed
Encourage all staff to stay, join in and endorse singing assemblies.	☐	☐
Create a collection of songs which celebrate festivals in various traditions.	☐	☐
Use action songs to get the whole school buzzing and motivated, including all abilities and levels of language.	☐	☐
Sing songs that tie in with positive citizenship and school values.	☐	☐
Encourage classes to take it in turns teaching the whole school their favourite songs.	☐	☐

Other ideas

Do families and visitors have opportunities to participate in the school's singing activities?

Singing Schools tell us that singing has become an important part of their identity and culture that pupils' families and school visitors enjoy and admire. Pupils and staff feel proud of their school and are pleased with what they have achieved together.

	In progress	Completed
Place copies of your Singing Schools Pledge Certificate* around the school.	☐	☐
Write to parents to let them know about the plan to become a Singing School.	☐	☐
Report on progress being made in the school newsletter and on the school website.	☐	☐
Invite parents to singing events throughout the year.	☐	☐
Incorporate singing into school events, such as sports day and evening concerts.	☐	☐
Start a parent and child weekly singing session for families before school.	☐	☐

Other ideas

* Downloadable from the product page on fabermusicstore.com

Going for Gold!

As we've said, being a Singing School is about being on a journey – one of progression, development and improvement. Even once you have got lots of singing happening there will always be areas where you can improve, include more children, broaden the repertoire and singing styles, and enhance leadership skills among staff and pupils. As you progress from Silver to Gold level you will be looking to take everything up a notch and increase the quality, breadth and reach of singing in your school.

Pupils' singing activity

Do pupils sing every day in a variety of contexts?

At Silver level all your pupils will be singing more than twice a week, both in and out of music lessons. At Gold level you would expect singing to be firmly rooted in all your class music lessons in support of instrumental, listening and creative work and also be happening for every child, every day in a variety of other contexts. How many of these have you achieved? (You don't need to do all of them.)

	In progress	Completed
Class music lesson	☐	☐
Singing in other subjects or topics	☐	☐
Regular assembly singing	☐	☐
Playground singing	☐	☐
Whole class instrumental work including singing	☐	☐
A choir	☐	☐
A school musical production	☐	☐
Other ideas		

Are pupils supported to lead singing and vocal work?

Building on pupils sharing their singing with others and suggesting songs they'd like to sing at school at Silver level, at Gold level pupils can begin to lead singing and vocal work themselves.

	In progress	Completed
Have children lead song learning (echo songs are great for first timers).	☐	☐
Develop a Young Singing Leaders project.	☐	☐
Create a 'lucky-dip song bag' which you fill with the names of known songs or song props. Children take it in turns to pull out a lucky-dip song and lead the singing.	☐	☐
Other ideas		

Do pupils practise ways to improve their singing?

At Silver level pupils are able to identify ways they can improve their singing. At Gold level they are able to practise ways to make those improvements. They will know how to go about making improvements to their singing without too much prompting from the singing leader, and improvements will then be evident.

	In progress	Completed

Make video or audio recordings of a performance and discuss it with the children.

Consider questions like:

- Could you hear all of the words?

- If there are actions, are they done well and is it appropriate?

- Can you hear all the parts, are they well balanced?

- Are all the parts accurately sung?
  (They will need help with focussed listening for this.)

- What do you think would have improved the performance?

When teaching a song, ask your pupils for ideas about how to perform the song.

Consider questions like:

- What is the song about?

- What do you think is the most important phrase or section in this song and why?

- How can you sing the song so that the listener understands the story?

- How could you use your voice to express the emotion of the song?

- Should any of the verses be sung differently? In a group? As a solo?

- Should there be any actions?

Other ideas

Do pupils sing in a range of ways and styles including creating original music with their voices?

As pupils develop vocally, we want them to be able to sing in more than one style of music, with a variety of tonal qualities to suit the mood and style of the music. As they develop musically, it's good to be exposed to a variety of genres so they can develop an understanding and appreciation of a wide range of types of music. A big part of understanding and enjoying music of different styles and genres is learning to 'tune-in' to it. Although the styles of music commonly used in popular culture are very familiar, other styles won't be, but can be tuned-in to, understood and enjoyed with a bit of exposure to them. One of the best ways to help young musicians to tune-in to different styles of music is for them to sing or play it. Listening is good too, but actively singing or playing the music builds stronger neural connections and helps the brain understand what is going on melodically and harmonically.

We also want our young singers to be experimenting creatively and inventing their own original music using their voices. Inventing songs, perhaps based on a familiar starting point, come very naturally to young children and it's a skill we don't want them to lose as they grow up. And the greater variety of musical styles they are familiar with, the more interesting and creative their invented songs will be. It's a bit like learning to write text in different styles, if you read different styles of writing you tune-into the language and are better equipped to write creatively and flexibly with imagination. So balance pupils being able to choose songs with some suggestions of your own which you think they will like, and will broaden their musical horizons and stretch their imaginations.

	In progress	Completed
Create a choir and involve pupils in choosing repertoire.	☐	☐
Select or create a school song, hymn or anthem.	☐	☐
In music lessons write songs, compose with the voice, e.g. composing riffs and layering them up based on pentatonic scales.	☐	☐
Teach the class songs from all over the world and let pupils from different countries or cultures teach new songs.	☐	☐
Choose repertoire from a broad range of musical styles for listening to in assemblies, and music lessons.	☐	☐

Other ideas

Staff singing activity

Do staff sing weekly, including the senior leadership team?

In a Singing School, you want all your staff, including the senior leadership team, to be modelling the behaviour that you are wanting from your pupils – enjoying singing together regularly.

	In progress	Completed
Make it routine for staff to sing together at the beginning of staff meetings.	☐	☐
Inspire staff to enjoy assembly singing by selecting songs they also like to sing,	☐	☐
Start a staff or community choir and have a performance goal in mind.	☐	☐
Take the school by surprise by organising a staff flashmob or staff-only performance within a school assembly or concert.	☐	☐

Other ideas

Are three or more staff leading singing at least twice a week and developing their confidence?

Ideally you would want all class teachers to be leading singing with their classes on a regular basis – hopefully every day. But of course some teachers will find it challenging to lead singing if they are not confident singers themselves and feel they lack the skills or knowledge to do it well. If your school has at least three staff regularly leading singing, you can build out from that over time, and it means that singing is pretty well embedded and will still happen even if you leave the school or are off sick. Developing teachers' confidence is absolutely key. Starting with something simple, sung in a group is a good first step, and gradually, with support and encouragement, confidence will build. What you're trying to build in your school is a culture where it is just normal for everyone to sing. Then the pupils won't be nervous or anxious about it and everyone will have a great time.

	In progress	Completed
Remind staff to use songs to help support their curriculum and help with school routine.	☐	☐
Write an action plan with the staff on how to develop confidence in singing and leading singing.	☐	☐

Other ideas

Do staff identify strategies to improve the quality of singing?

At Gold level, staff should be able to begin to identify what needs improving in relation to the quality of the singing and know how to go about improving it. This links to staff guiding pupils through a reflective questioning process, helping them to identify areas for improvement (see Chapter 9, page 125) so a good starting point is for staff to be asking themselves some of these same reflective questions. Following the principles set out in the Vocal Leader Checklist will help staff with this. You could also seek some external input from vocal leaders outside the school, who might be able to come in and lead a session with the pupils from which both pupils and staff can learn how to improve their singing.

	In progress	Completed
Create a poster for the staffroom to let all staff know how they can improve the quality of singing and creative vocal work.	☐	☐
Teach staff a new range of physical and vocal warm-ups to use in class or assembly.	☐	☐
Refresh or update staff knowledge of vocal health by inviting a vocal leader into a staff meeting.	☐	☐
Other ideas		

Do staff singing leaders model and share good vocal practice with colleagues?

The Vocal Leader Checklist will be helpful to you here, as will Chapter 4 on Vocal Leadership.

	In progress	Completed
Put together a song playlist (with help from colleagues) for all staff to use with their classes.	☐	☐
Get together with other teachers and singing leaders.	☐	☐
Start a music network meeting for local teachers if there isn't one already.	☐	☐
Pair up confident singing leaders with those who are less confident.	☐	☐
Other ideas		

Senior leadership team and governors' involvement

Are the senior leadership team and governors involved in the Singing School process and are they actively supporting staff and pupils to develop as singers and vocal leaders?

Building on their endorsement of and commitment to the school's decision to become a Singing School, as Singing School Coordinator you will need to keep them engaged and informed of progress to maintain their enthusiasm and keep it on their radar.

	In progress	Completed
Get the senior leadership team to attend singing assemblies and to join in the singing with the children.	☐	☐
Encourage the senior leadership team to support staff in introducing songs in staff meetings.	☐	☐
Invite the senior leadership team and governors to events where singing may take place.	☐	☐
Suggest that the senior leadership team contribute to leading singing in the classroom.	☐	☐

Other ideas

Do the senior leadership team and governors demonstrate continued whole school support and encourage further development for school singing?

	In progress	Completed
Ask the senior leadership team and governors to write news stories on the website or in the newsletter about the school's journey towards becoming a Singing School.	☐	☐
Encourage them to get in touch with local media (e.g. local radio and newspapers) to highlight the singing achievements of the school.	☐	☐
Ask them to support teacher CPD and attendance at courses.	☐	☐

Other ideas

Whole school community involvement

Does communal singing mark significant moments of school life and do families and visitors share in this?

	In progress	Completed
Use songs to mark the major festivals such as Harvest, Christmas, Diwali, Hanukkah, Chinese New Year.	☐	☐
Create a playlist of songs that can be used to celebrate achievement such as Prize-giving ceremonies or Leavers' Assemblies/events.	☐	☐
Connect with other local schools for joint singing events, particularly senior schools that pupils may be moving onto.	☐	☐
Introduce a welcome song for new children arriving at the school.	☐	☐
Organise a themed-week and incorporate sharing songs and song performances into this.	☐	☐
Get involved with singing in the wider community, through school singing festivals, performing at a local care home, encouraging children to join their local choirs or after-school/holiday singing clubs.	☐	☐
Connect with other schools to learn about each other's singing activity.	☐	☐

Other ideas

11

WHAT NEXT? REVIEWING THE PLAN AND KEEPING IT ON TRACK: PLATINUM

Your school, with your guidance and encouragement, has committed to investing in singing as a way of changing or enhancing the culture of the school. This isn't something that you 'arrive at' and then stop. It is an ongoing process of commitment, learning and development over time. You will always have new pupils entering the school, new staff joining and there will always be more that can be done to keep moving forward.

What could you be aiming for next? And how might you go about creating the next plan? What's the ongoing legacy of all that you've achieved up until this point? And how can your school singing get even better?

That's what we're going to think about in this final chapter – future-proofing and giving lasting resilience to your school's singing strategy.

Future-proofing

Any strategy needs regular review and monitoring to ensure that it is keeping on track. Think about how regularly you want your school to be doing this in relation to singing and how you will measure and track progress.

Consider, as well, ongoing CPD and skill development within the staff team, just as you would for any aspect of teaching practice. And you will want to ensure that as staff and pupils move on over time, there is sufficient resilience and commitment right across the school to enable singing to continue to be a key area of focus and source of pride for the school.

To begin with, think about these questions in relation to your particular school and where you are currently in your Singing School journey:

- What's the current skills level across staff in the school?
- How frequently would you think it necessary to do a singing skills audit to see where opportunities for development might be?
- How might the school commit to ongoing CPD and training for new and current staff?
- What will happen when key staff leave and new staff join the school?
- How might recruitment of new staff help you to develop your skills base across the school?
- What role might partnerships with other schools and organisations play for your school's singing in the future?

- How is your school described to the outside world and what is the position of its commitment to singing within that description?
- How has, or how might the school's commitment to excellence in singing change the way your school is perceived in the wider community and the reputation of your school?

Platinum Singing Schools

Being a Platinum Singing School is about your school's readiness to be an 'Ambassador Singing School' through the quality of your school's singing and singing leadership. Also, the provision you make for all pupils to fully participate and make progress and how you can provide an example of best practice for other schools.

Singing will have been fully embedded within the school for some time. Singing will likely have made some significant differences to the school's culture, the school's community, it's success in learning outcomes and the lives of the children it serves. The singing you have going on will be of a consistently high standard across the whole school, and the vocal leadership too will be consistently of a high quality. Let's consider how you might take your Singing School towards Platinum Level.

Pupils' singing activity

Do pupils enjoy singing over a sustained period of time, including through passages of transition, demonstrating progress?

At Gold level singing has become firmly rooted in all your class music lessons in support of instrumental, listening and creative work and is also happening for every child, every day in a variety of other contexts. At Platinum level, you will have absorbed and acted upon the learnings from Chapter 9 on making progress and improving singing, and it will be the norm for singing to be a regular part of a pupil's school life from when they first arrive at the school through transitions to different year-groups and key stages. It will be noticeable that the children's musical and vocal ability is progressing over time.

You may also be thinking about preparation for the transition to secondary school and perhaps, where this is possible, planning singing-based transition projects which ease the transition and give the music teacher in the secondary school the ability to provide some continuity of musical experience when the students first arrive in their new school.

> "In Platinum schools there is a sense that this technical foundation had become so firmly embedded as to be automatic and natural."
>
> Sing Up Awards – A Qualitative Evaluation, 2011

	In progress	Completed
Songs have been embedded within school life and are used across the school every day.	☐	☐
Pupils are supported in the transition from one stage of school life to the next to encourage them to keep singing.	☐	☐
The musical and vocal progression of pupils is measured and tracked.	☐	☐
Arrangements are made for succession planning among staff and ensuring continuity of singing in the school in the event of key staff leaving.	☐	☐
Singing expertise is spread across the whole staff.	☐	☐

Other ideas

Do pupils show an independence and spontaneity in singing leadership both in and outside the classroom?

At Gold level, pupils have begun to lead singing and vocal work themselves. You have been using what you've learnt in Chapter 4 on vocal leadership and Young Singing Leaders and have been nurturing those skills too. At Platinum level this has become more established and children are regularly leading songs in a variety of contexts. They have developed some confidence in doing this and are able to lead singing independently and are sometimes doing this unprompted.

	In progress	Completed
Opportunities exist for children to lead singing in the playground and they are doing this of their own accord.	☐	☐
Pupils regularly lead singing in the classroom, as well as in assembly and in concerts.	☐	☐
Older pupils support younger children with their singing activity.	☐	☐
The developing skills of Young Singing Leaders are recognised and there's a structure of recognition in the school for your Young Singing Leaders' scheme.	☐	☐

Other ideas

Do pupils develop confidence and understanding and model ways to improve their singing?

At Gold level, pupils are able to practise ways to make improvements in their singing. At Platinum level, they will be more able to develop their own singing without guidance or with minimal guidance. They will be independently spotting what improvements can be made and be able to suggest and practise ways of making those improvements, e.g. through 'break it down, slow it down' techniques and other approaches suggested in Chapter 9.

	In progress	Completed
There are opportunities for pupils to reflect on their singing and to recognise and articulate what improvements could be made.	☐	☐
Children model ways to improve their own singing, for example, by leading a warm-up, demonstrating good posture, singing with an unforced sound.	☐	☐
Children express themselves clearly through singing.	☐	☐

Other ideas

Do pupils experience a diverse range of high-quality singing opportunities in and outside the school, and are they supported to extend their interests?

At Gold level, pupils have already been singing in a range of styles and have been developing their creativity with their voices through simple song writing and improvising. This will have given them a flavour of the wide range of types of singing and musical activity they could pursue. At Platinum level, they will be progressing with these, both in and outside of school and be further supported to extend and develop their singing and musical experiences and competencies.

	In progress	Completed
There are opportunities in school for pupils to participate in; and listen to, music of a high quality in a range of genres.	☐	☐
Opportunities are available for pupils after school to take part in extra-curricular activity, get involved with local festivals, singing events and visit concerts.	☐	☐
You know of and can signpost children who want to progress further to local or regional singing opportunities.	☐	☐

Other ideas

Staff singing activity

Are staff advocates for singing?

At Gold level, you will have all staff singing at least weekly and three or more staff leading singing at least twice a week. By the time you have really embedded this across the school, at Platinum level, staff right across the school should be firm advocates for singing. They will have witnessed the change to the school and the pupils' experience of being in school as a result of singing – they may well have experienced some change in themselves.

	In progress	Completed
Staff advocates for singing are recognised and valued and encouraged to spread it further.	☐	☐
All staff encourage pupils to take part in and improve their singing.	☐	☐
Opportunities exist for staff to share the benefits of singing that they and their pupils have experienced with each other, pupils and parents/carers and Governors.	☐	☐
Staff get involved and help with singing events or performances.	☐	☐
There is a staff choir, who involve the school and wider community in their performances.	☐	☐

Other ideas

Are all staff involved in leading singing?

At Gold level, three or more staff have been leading singing at least twice a week and developing their confidence. At Platinum level, you will have worked with your colleagues to cascade skills and expertise right across the staff team so that every member of staff is able to be involved in leading singing in some way. Some may just be leading singing in the classroom, others will have developed the confidence to lead singing in other contexts – like in assembly. You might have playground supervisors leading singing at break-time.

	In progress	Completed
All teachers are using singing within their classrooms and are encouraged to develop and spread their practices more widely.	☐	☐
Some teachers are now confident to lead singing outside of their classroom context, perhaps with larger groups of pupils and you are aware of the factors which have enabled them to make that progress.	☐	☐
Staff currently help with school performances, concerts or singing events outside of school and you are looking to expand upon or share this more widely.	☐	☐

Other ideas

Do staff develop inspirational singing activity in and beyond the school through collaboration and partnership, signposting pupils to a range of opportunities?

One significant development that distinguishes Gold level and Platinum level is the extent to which schools become outward looking, expanding their vocal practice to connect with other schools and organisations. This will require strong collaborative working both within your school and with potential partners.

	In progress	Completed
The good practice already embedded within your school is spread to other neighbouring schools.	☐	☐
There are inspirational opportunities available through working in partnership with local, regional and national music and performing arts organisations.	☐	☐
Staff collaborate well within the school to put on singing events.	☐	☐
The school looks for funding to organise singing projects, perhaps in partnership with an expert provider.	☐	☐

Other ideas

Do all staff understand the importance of good vocal health and do they care for the voices of those they work with?

At Gold level, your staff singing leaders will have been modelling and sharing good vocal practice with their colleagues in order to spread knowledge and expertise more widely across the staff team. By Platinum level, the importance of good vocal health and how to care for the voice is understood by all staff.

	In progress	Completed
All staff members approach good vocal health in their lessons and this is consistent from one class to another.	☐	☐
CPD opportunities are available to staff in relation to developing their understanding and expertise of good vocal health and vocal leadership (perhaps run by yourself, using chapters 3 and 4 of this book).	☐	☐
Staff are given formal or informal opportunities to share ideas on good vocal health and vocal leadership, e.g. in staff meetings.	☐	☐
Vocal health knowledge is passed on to new staff when they join the school, perhaps as part of their induction process.	☐	☐

Other ideas

Senior leadership team and governors' involvement

Do the senior leadership team and governors champion and join in singing as a key part of school life?

At Gold level, the senior leadership team and governors are involved in the Singing School process and are actively supporting staff and pupils to develop as singers and vocal leaders. At Platinum level, this commitment from the senior management of the school has become further embedded and is demonstrated through their involvement in and championing of singing.

As Singing School Coordinator, you will have been working hard to keep them engaged and informed of progress and shining a light on what has been achieved. They've had plenty of opportunities to hear and see the singing happening in their school and have gained an understanding of how it is making a difference to the school. They should be able to articulate how singing is helping them to meet goals within the School Development Plan for example.

	In progress	Completed
Members of the senior leadership team and governors attend and join in with the singing in assembles and they encourage it to happen more frequently or with a wider range of personnel, i.e. it isn't always the head teacher and Chair of Governors only who come along and take part.	☐	☐
Structures are in place for the senior leadership team to give praise to children for their singing, perhaps through prize-giving or an awards system.	☐	☐
The senior leadership team champion singing. They are able to speak about it and its importance to the school at school events and concerts.	☐	☐
They lead singing themselves or are encouraged and supported to do so if they don't already.	☐	☐

Other ideas

Do the senior leadership team and governors advocate a range of approaches in using singing to benefit the school and the wider community?

This is about the depth and range of support that is available to you as Singing School Coordinator from the senior management of the school. Getting to this point, where you've got high level support for your work, will make it much easier for you to expand and develop the school's ongoing commitment to singing and to ensure that it is protected for the future even if key staff or senior management leave the school.

	In progress	Completed
Your school has ongoing commitment to training and CPD to support staff to develop their vocal leadership skills.	☐	☐
Senior managers are involved in organising music or singing events in and outside the school, for example with local schools, local music organisations etc.	☐	☐
Singing is embedded within school planning to support whole-school aims and objectives and within the wider curriculum. You no longer need to remind management to make this happen, it happens as a matter of course.	☐	☐
School systems and processes are in place to ensure that singing remains a key part of school life if key staff were to leave the school.	☐	☐

Other ideas

Whole school community involvement

Do staff and pupils find routes to enjoy singing, aspire to and achieve excellence and make progress in and outside of school?

	In progress	Completed
Consider the extra-curricular singing activities are pupils involved in and look to expand.	☐	☐
These opportunities are available for all pupils regardless of background or financial means. If not, you are considering how to create genuine equality of access.	☐	☐
Staff singing aspirations are being raised and met. They perform outside of school and partner with other local choirs.	☐	☐

Other ideas

Does the school have opportunities to hear and participate in singing outside the school and to experience a diverse range of singing?

	In progress	Completed
The whole school hear and participate in a diverse range of singing opportunities.	☐	☐
Outside concerts are attended, or visiting music groups come to the school to perform.	☐	☐
Opportunities exist for staff to share the benefits of singing that they and their pupils have experienced with each other, pupils and parents/carers and Governors.	☐	☐
Set up and run local charity or community concerts.	☐	☐
Outside opportunities are not just for the school choir but for the wider school community.	☐	☐

Other ideas

The Singing Ambassador School

Platinum Singing Schools act as advocates for singing outside of the school gates. They will:

	In progress	Completed
Have an outward focus, inspiring and connecting with the wider community. This might, for example, involve you organising a Big Sing event for local schools.	☐	☐
Support other schools on their own Singing School journey using your experience and knowledge to help them.	☐	☐
Link with local schools to continue developing Young Singing Leaders in their area – maybe a Young Singing Leaders exchange programme for example.	☐	☐
Set up collaborative performance opportunities for your school with others.	☐	☐

Other ideas

Troubleshooting

Some common questions and scenarios that we get asked about relate to things that can go wrong and knock a Singing School off-course. There are lots of pressures on schools and teachers to cover many bases and time is often limited within and around the school day. Here are the most common issues that tend to arise and some tips for dealing with them:

Our main singing leader has left the school – how do we keep the singing going?

It is very often the case that becoming a Singing School requires the energy and passion of one individual to make it happen, particularly to begin with. The idea with becoming a Singing School is that singing has become sufficiently embedded within the school that there are many other teachers or other staff who feel able and willing to pick up where your original singing leader has left off, however, if you feel you need an injection of expertise there are many ways to go about bringing that into the school either temporarily or on a regular basis. A combination of seeking an external expert through other local schools or music organisations plus getting some training for your remaining staff will soon bring the sparkle back to your singing. In England, try contacting your local Music Education Hub. They all have a local singing strategy and plans to engage schools in singing. They will also have local vocal experts working for them who can either lead singing in your school or lead some training for your staff.

We have a new head teacher and they need convincing about the value of singing in school.

As we've discussed earlier in the book, having the support of your head teacher is vital if you are going to embed singing right across the school and make it part of the school's culture. If you've already gone some way towards becoming a Singing School before your new head teacher arrives you should have some singing happening and some evidence that you can take to them to demonstrate what value it is bringing to the school. You will hopefully also have some allies on the rest of the staff team and among the school governors and parents. You can also go back to Chapter 1 and use the research evidence to make your case for singing remaining a priority. Good luck!

We have a wonderful school choir but many of the older pupils are due to leave at the end of the year, how can I keep it going?

We hear this a lot from teachers and it is always a sad moment when talented older pupils leave the school. Hopefully, you will have younger pupils who will get a chance to step up and have their moment to shine, even if they're not quite ready yet, you can work with them to encourage their confidence and talents for the future. You can also be working with the younger children and using your growing experience and leadership skills to develop them as singers too. Some pupils will need to be encouraged to take these opportunities, so try not to rely on the same small group of confident singers to take solos. If you have a good relationship with your local secondary schools you can arrange some cross-over singing events or singing festivals so that your younger pupils can hear what their older role models have gone on to achieve in secondary school. This will be really inspiring for them.

Exams are coming up and I'm being told there's no time for singing

There are huge pressures on pupils in the run-up to exams and sometimes it can seem like time spent singing isn't the priority. However, singing is a great stress buster, and can relieve tension at high-pressure moments and it will be a really healthy release for pupils to spend some time singing during these periods in their lives. Remind other teachers (and parents) about the physiological and emotional benefits of singing and of how singing activates the brain like no other activity.

Pupil attainment has dipped in our school and I'm being told we need to focus on 'core' subjects

Similar to the exam-time problem, a renewed focus on learning outcomes for pupils shouldn't mean the side-lining of singing in your school – quite the opposite in fact. Many schools have actually used their singing to boost learning outcomes and directly attribute their academic results to the fact that singing and music are woven through the fabric of the school. Make these points to the school leadership team, show them the evidence and if possible, get them to speak to other schools who have taken this approach. It really does work!

Endnotes

[1] For more information and to see the research, visit www.singup.org/research

[2] See K. Menehan, *Singing and the brain* (www.chorusamerica.org) to read about results of MRI scans of singers' brains.

[3] A. Barker, *Can music change our immune system?* www.britishscienceassociation.org/blog

[4] G. Welch, *The Benefits of Singing for Adolescents* (Institute of Education, 2011) Available at www.singup.org.

[5] C. Sheppard, *The Neuroscience of Singing* (2016) https://upliftconnect.com/neuroscience-of-singing and G. Welch and E. Himonides, *Researching the second year of the National Singing Programme in England: An ongoing impact evaluation of children's singing behaviour and identity* (Institute of Education, 2009)

[6] For more information, see: E. Pearce, J. Launay, and R. Dunbar, *The ice-breaker effect: singing mediates fast social bonding* (The Royal Society, 2015)

[7] Extracts from *Singing in the Lower Secondary School* by Martin Ashley © Oxford University Press 2015. Reproduced by permission of Oxford University Press. All rights reserved.

[8] For more information see Cambiata Institute at www.cambiata.music.unt.edu

[9] For more information, see: Lynne Gackle, *Finding Ophelia's Voice, Opening Ophelia's Heart: Nurturing the Adolescent Female Voice: An Exploration of the Physiological, Psychological, and Musical Development of Female Students* (Heritage, 2011)

[10] C. Burton-Hill, *What do conductors actually do* (BBC culture, online) and I. Hewett *What do conductors do?* (Daily Telegraph, online, 2014)

[11] O. Sacks, *Musicophilia* (Picador, 2008)

[12] R. Bunting, *Muslim Music and Culture in the Curriculum* (Birmingham Advisory and Support Service, 2006)

[13] Visit excathedra.co.uk to discover Ex Cathedra's Singing Playgrounds project.

[14] With special thanks to Jenni Parkinson, Sophie Gray, Aimee Toshney and Emily Tully for their help and expertise.

[15] Written through interview with Lucinda Bristow.

[16] See The British Kodály Academy (britishkodalyacademy.org) for more information.